Design Your Happy Healthy Wealthy Life

The Ultimate
9 Week Planner

GINA PIGOTT

RED PENGUIN Books

The Ultimate 9 Week Planner

Copyright © 2021 by Gina Pigott

All rights reserved

Editors Noelle Grassel and Jennifer Varenka

Published by Red Penguin Books

Bellerose Village, New York

Library of Congress Control Number: 2021900225

ISBN

Print 978-1-63777-009-2

Digital 978-1-63777-010-8

To Paulie
who supports me in everything I do
no matter what ...

♡

with Love,
Humor, Positivity, and
Unwavering Belief and Dedication

To my Mom
who so kindly inserted the memetic that

♡

"I can do anything"
and
"It's all about my choices!"

ACKNOWLEDGEMENTS

To Jim Bunch
My Coach, Mentor and Partner. Thank you for teaching me and for
creating a program that gives everyone in this game we call life the
ability to level up and transform their lives in just 9 weeks,
giving them the path to design and live their Ultimate Life.

The Ultimate Team - Fran, Charlie, JV, Mary and Noelle
You are the magic behind the curtain that makes everything look easy!
... and I am eternally grateful.

**The Ultimate 9 Week Planner is available in a variety of file formats,
and integrates well with your digital devices using GoodNotes
for a seamless, interactive experience.**

**Contact info@bestdamnsuccesssystem.com
for additional formats so that YOU can carry
The Ultimate 9 Week Planner with you wherever you go,
and for more information on coaching and programs.**

WELCOME!

You are playing the Happy Healthy Wealthy Game
and are now on the path to creating your Ultimate Life.

I couldn't be more excited that you are reading this and using my planner to assist you in designing your Ultimate Life! Before you get started with your Planner, I would like to tell you my story and why I believe from my nose to my toes this is the best system ever created.

After running multiple companies and businesses for others, I created a Dream Team that grew into an enormous global business, creating jobs and helping independent partners create the life they desire. It was great for a while, and then it wasn't.

I realized that having extreme success and wealth doesn't make life great.

Money, over time, family and health, isn't wealth at all.

So, I made a decision 6 years ago to change my life and follow my passion. I was ready and wanted to step back and enjoy my family, my environment and my life.

And the man that started me down this road and with whom I now partner is **Jim Bunch! Jim and The Ultimate Game of Life (TUG)** helped me level up my game and reach levels of success I never dreamed were possible. The Game not only teaches, what I feel, are some of the most important lessons to lead a happy, healthy and wealthy life, additionally, the platform itself has accountability to create the habits that drive the highest levels of success; more than any program I have ever seen. It addresses ALL 9 environments in my life to help me seek out balance and not just to look to achieve, grabbing the brass ring at all costs. I have now come full circle and have joined Jim and Ultimate Life as a Player, Coach, and CEO! I am overjoyed with the plans we have in store for the universe to make this planet a better place for all!

So...Here I am... I took the leap and am not looking back! I made the decision to focus on helping others with their success and to give back what was given to me from all the wonderful people (too many to mention here) with whom I've had the pleasure of sharing this ride.

I have a Vision of everyone on the planet
rocking life and coming together to create a better world.

I am on a Mission to create a path for people to **GET PUMPED**
to reach their wildest dreams and live their Ultimate Life!

What's YOUR why?
What are YOUR dreams?
What's the first choice YOU are going to make
and turn your dreams into reality?

LET'S FIND OUT TOGETHER!

I can't wait to meet you and enjoy the
journey in this wonderful life together.
Thanks for joining me for this Ultimate Life adventure
The Happy Healthy Wealthy 9 Week Challenge!

Let's Rock and Roll.
Game on!

contents

01 HOW TO PLAY & WIN THE GAME OF LIFE

"The Game is Always On!
The only way to lose the Game is to quit."

~ Jim Bunch

week one

week one

HOW TO PLAY AND WIN THE GAME OF LIFE

_____

_____

_____

_____

_____

_____

_____

_____

_____

_____

_____

_____

_____

_____

_____

_____

_____

_____

_____

_____

_____

_____

_____

_____

INTRODUCTION 01

As you are playing this level of the Game, you will be creating the habits that will help you WIN in "The Ultimate Game of Life," which means more Happiness, better Health and more Wealth.

This level is also known as "The Happy Healthy Wealthy Game" (HHW) because it helps you redesign and refocus your life around what's important to you, what makes you truly Happy, Healthy and Wealthy. We call this your "Trilogy Score."

The Game provides you a snapshot of your life in 9 weeks or less and it reflects how you play the Game of Life and why you are getting the results you are (both positive and negative).

The Trilogy Score is made up of your:
Happiness
Health
Wealth

THE 3 A'S

01

The Game is designed to raise your AWARENESS to your daily thoughts, feelings, habits & actions.

You will become more aware as you take 3 DAILY ACTIONS toward your goals. The environments of the Game will be working on you internally and externally to hold you ACCOUNTABLE TO YOUR DAILY COMMITMENTS while reprogramming you for Ultimate Success (aka: Happiness, Health & Wealth). This is what we refer to as "The 3 A's" (Awareness, Action & Accountability).

At the end of the Game, you will have the necessary Skillsets, Mindset & Environments to continue setting and achieving personal goals throughout the rest of your life no matter how big of a Game you decide to play.

The 3 A's for the Game:

Awareness

Action

Accountability

8 KEY
PRINCIPLES OF
THE GAME

Principle I
The Game is Always On™

How we do games is often how we do life, and how we do anything is how we do everything.

The HHW Game provides you with a snapshot of your life and shows you the truth behind your thoughts, feelings and actions as you move toward your goals.

Your beliefs, rules, and habits will stand out more clearly as your awareness rises and you take daily actions. Keep in mind changing may bring up a variety of emotions: doubt, elation, anger, resistance, joy or other reactions. This is all part of the Game; embrace it fully.

Being transparent and authentic will accelerate your success in the Game, so be sure to "tell it like it is—Not better, Not worse" than it is.

Tracking your performance using the Scorecard, journaling, blogging, etc. is a valuable tool for reflection and course correction. We often say, "You won't improve what you aren't willing to measure."

Remember that asking for help is not a sign of weakness, it's a sign of strength, and it gives others the opportunity to feel good about helping you.

Principle 2
Be a Pro Player

In sports, there are levels of the game coinciding with your abilities. Amateur, College, Semi-Pro and Professional. If you make it to the very top, you are considered an All-Star Player. To reach the highest level of any game, you must practice 100% Responsibility. 99% is actually harder than 100% because you haven't fully engaged in your goal.

In life there are 4 levels of the Game. Identify which level you are in for each of the 3 areas of Happiness, Health & Wealth and set your target to reach the next level during the Challenge.

Level 1: Repair and Recovery – This is the level with a sub-zero score. In Wealth, it equates with debt. In Health, it equates to disease and illness. In Happiness, it equates with sadness or confusion.

Level 2: Foundation - At this level, we create building blocks for sustainable change. We determine what people, resources and strategies are needed to bring fulfillment, and go about securing them.

Level 3: Reserves - This is the first level of abundance and attraction, where more than enough exists of what you desire and need. You get to do what you want, when you want, with whom you want.

Level 4: Mastery/Enlightenment – Enlightenment is defined as a life that is completely conscious, completely on purpose. At Level 4, you are empowered, inspired and completely present in each moment. Your experience of life is one of flow and ease.

A considerable amount of effort is required to rise from Level 1 to Level 2 in any of the 3 life areas. After Level 2 is attained, getting to Levels 3 and 4 requires much less exertion.

Principle 3

Play Full Out & Play to Win

Even pro athletes don't compete on the field every day, all day. They understand, to reach peak performance on game days, they must take time to plan and prepare, practice their game plan, relax and recharge their bodies and minds…. then on game day, give it 100%.

In the Ultimate Game, we want you to take time out like the pros, by setting your goals, planning your day the night before and taking 3 daily actions to move you closer to your Happiness, Health & Wealth Goals.

*** One key point to remember - play full out but never play to the point of burn out. Playing too hard, too long can lead to mental, emotional and physical depletion and eventually put you on the bench or injured reserve. It's okay to take time out of the Game, even quit for today…as long as you start up again tomorrow. Set aside time to Relax, Recharge, Refocus, Recommit, Restart.*

PLAYING FULL OUT TO ME IS …

_____

_____

_____

_____

_____

_____

Principle 4

Take Risks, Never Be AT Risk

The whole purpose of the Game is to challenge yourself to break through your barriers, reach new highs and shatter old records of what you thought was possible....in other words, take risks.

That being said, we want to remind you that you should never put yourself at risk in the Game. Seek the advice of professionals before starting any physical activity or making financial decisions putting you at risk.

REFLECTION

Risks I've taken that have paid off?

_____

_____

_____

Risks I'd like to take?

_____

_____

_____

What have I done that put me at risk?

_____

_____

_____

What did I learn?

_____

_____

_____

Life is a Team Sport™ Principle 5

Anyone who has created success knows it's up to them to create their own Happiness, Health & Wealth but it can't be done alone. Collaboration is an important element of the Game; it will accelerate your success when you grab a hand-up and lend a hand-out.

We are all in the game of life together and we can all win. There are unlimited resources available to you inside and outside the Game, and if we understand the key to reaching any goal is to harness the power of People, Ideas, and Resources, we can achieve any goal.

MY TEAM

PERSONAL

_____

_____

_____

PROFESSIONAL

_____

_____

_____

Principle 6

Everything is an Environment & Environments are Everything

Consider for a moment everything you can see, hear, taste, touch, and even the intangible things you can't, are environments. Each of the things in your life impacts your thoughts, feelings and actions in a positive and inspiring way or a negative and draining way.

Environments play a major role in our ability to succeed, and when properly designed, they can facilitate ease and flow in our lives and even "partner with us in our goals." When environments are done by "default" instead of by "design," people experience drag, resistance and struggle in pursuit of their goals.

In the Game, we want you to ADD environments that Inspire you, DELETE the ones that Expire you (drain) and SHIFT or upgrade the ones which need fine-tuning.

We will cover this in detail in Module 5, so for the time being, start with making some improvements to the easy environments like Physical, Body or Financial.

TAKE THE ULTIMATE LIFE 9 ENVIRONMENTS ASSESSMENT

Simplicity Succeeds™

Let's face it, for most people in the modern world, life is way too busy as it is. In the Game, we'd like you to craft a winning game plan, which includes doing less and being more. The first place to start is with your goals.

Simplifying your goals and your Game includes getting clear on what you want, making decisions, and taking actions to move toward the 3 goals you've set. Don't over-complicate the Game. Put your Happiness first, then Health, then Wealth and watch what happens to the quality of your life.

Deciding where to focus is easy; just remember the phrase "Stop, Start, Continue." "Stop" doing the things you know you shouldn't be doing. "Start" doing the things you should, and "Continue" doing the things that are working.

STOP/START/CONTINUE

Things I'd like to stop doing

_____

_____

Things I'd like to start doing

_____

_____

Things I'd like to continue doing

_____

_____

Principle 8

Celebrate Everything... Often

This Challenge naturally attracts over-achievers who want more out of life. Trust me, I get it. What I also know is, we are the same people who constantly achieve and never feel fulfilled.

Take a few minutes every day to capture your wins, accomplishments, progress, insights and awarenesses in the App and this Planner. If you continue to achieve without rewarding yourself, how fun is the Game going to be?

On the flip side, while capturing our wins is important, it's also equally as valuable to "Learn from our Losses." In pro sports, if you have a losing season, at least that season will end and you can regroup, re-strategize, bring in the proper resources and set yourself up to win.

In other words, you leave the bad season behind and prepare for a winning season. In life, people often drag a losing season into a losing lifetime and they never learn from the hurdles and roadblocks, they just keep on beating their heads against the wall year after year.

SUCCESSES TO CELEBRATE

_____

_____

_____

_____

_____

_____

challenge
week one

HOW TO PLAY & WIN THE GAME: THE STRUCTURE OF THE ULTIMATE GAME OF LIFE

Set & Achieve 3 Inspiring Goals:

You will create 3 goals for the 9 weeks (1 Happy, 1 Healthy, 1 Wealthy Goal). The goals should be authentic and inspiring to you. You will likely modify the goals as the Game goes along so don't worry about getting them 100% right at the start.

Plan your day the night before -

Commit to 3 Daily Habits to earn 3 points/day:

Every weekday, Monday through Friday, you will "commit" to a total of 3 daily habits the night before. You can commit to more than 3 but the key is to complete all the habits you commit to each day or you get ZERO points for the day. You will start by creating 5 to 7 daily habits in each section (Happy, Healthy, Wealthy) and put them on your Scorecard so it's easy to know what to commit to each day.

Track your Daily Points on the Scorecard and in the App:

To qualify for daily points, you must commit to and complete at least one habit per HHW category, per day and track it on your Scorecard and share in the App. Each Scorecard habit that is completed will earn 1 point. And each win shared in the App will earn you much, much more and get you on the Leaderboard. You can earn additional bonus points for each additional bonus action you achieve, as long as you completed the 3 habits you committed to for that day. If you commit to any habit and don't achieve it before going to bed, you get ZERO points for the day, no matter how many other bonus actions you completed.

challenge
week one

Proprietary Scorecard System:

The Scorecard system is designed to keep you on track, focused and highly aware of your true behaviors.

The Scorecard is designed to help you track & measure your daily and weekly progress by keeping accurate records of your daily points. It will also assist you in becoming clear on your 3 goals and 3 daily habits while checking in internally with whether you are "inspired" or "expired" by the pursuit of your goals. It's also a support tool to remind you to celebrate your daily accomplishments.

Remember, "You can only improve what you can measure," and if you are resisting change, it will show up here because results don't lie ☺.

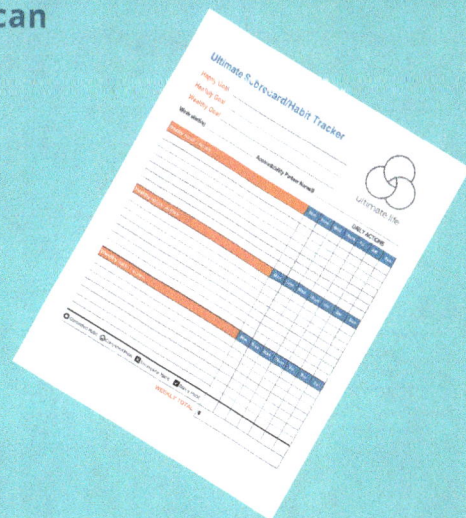

Scorecard / Habit Tracker

Happy Goal _____

Healthy Goal _____

Wealthy Goal _____

Week starting _____ Accountability Partner Name/# _____

ultimate life

DAILY ACTIONS

Happy Habits / Actions	Mon	Tues	Wed	Thurs	Fri
_____					
_____					
_____					
_____					
_____					
_____					
_____					

Healthy Habits / Actions	Mon	Tues	Wed	Thurs	Fri
_____					
_____					
_____					
_____					
_____					
_____					
_____					

Wealthy Habits / Actions	Mon	Tues	Wed	Thurs	Fri
_____					
_____					
_____					
_____					
_____					
_____					
_____					

⚙ Committed Habit ☺ Completed Habit ☒ Incomplete Habit ☑ Bonus Habit

WEEKLY TOTAL | **0**

AFFIRMATIONS

Power Up

Date ___ / ___
SMTWTFS

TODAY'S MANTRA

TODAY'S THOUGHTS

_____
_____
_____
_____
_____
_____
_____
_____
_____

BRIGHT IDEAS

_____
_____
_____
_____

3 Commitments	Habits	How I Will Lead
H:	Start:	Myself:
H:	Stop:	
		Others:
W:	Continue:	

"You were born to win."
~ Zig Ziglar

TOP 3 PRIORITIES

Power Play

CALLS:

To make   To return

1.

2.

3.

Date ___ / ___
SMTWTFS

6:00	_____	1:00	_____
6:30	_____	1:30	_____
7:00	_____	2:00	_____
7:30	_____	2:30	_____
8:00	_____	3:00	_____
8:30	_____	3:30	_____
9:00	_____	4:00	_____
9:30	_____	4:30	_____
10:00	_____	5:00	_____
10:30	_____	5:30	_____
11:00	_____	6:00	_____
11:30	_____	6:30	_____
12:00	_____	7:00	_____
12:30	_____	7:30	_____

Impact   Opportunity   Connection

Stay hydrated!

Step goal: _____   Steps completed: _____   Movement goal: _____

NOTES

_____

_____

_____

_____

_____

_____

_____

_____

_____

_____

_____

_____

_____

_____

_____

_____

_____

_____

_____

_____

_____

To Do	Shopping List	Appointments to Make

Power Down

GRATITUDE

NAILED IT!

REFLECTION

_____
_____
_____
_____
_____
_____
_____
_____
_____
_____

AWARENESS

_____
_____
_____
_____

Commitments Completed	Today's Wins	My HHW Score & Why
H:		H: 1 2 3 4 5
		_____
		_____
H:		H: 1 2 3 4 5
		_____
		_____
W:		W: 1 2 3 4 5
		_____
		_____
		Daily Total: _____

AFFIRMATIONS

Power Up

Date ___ / ___
SMTWTFS

TODAY'S MANTRA

TODAY'S THOUGHTS

_____
_____
_____
_____
_____
_____
_____
_____
_____
_____

BRIGHT IDEAS

_____
_____
_____
_____

3 Commitments	Habits	How I Will Lead
H:	Start:	Myself:
H:	Stop:	Others:
W:	Continue:	

The Game is a giant mirror.

TOP 3 PRIORITIES

Power Play

CALLS:
To make   To return

1.

2.

3.

Date ___ / ___
SMTWTFS

6:00 _____	1:00 _____
6:30 _____	1:30 _____
7:00 _____	2:00 _____
7:30 _____	2:30 _____
8:00 _____	3:00 _____
8:30 _____	3:30 _____
9:00 _____	4:00 _____
9:30 _____	4:30 _____
10:00 _____	5:00 _____
10:30 _____	5:30 _____
11:00 _____	6:00 _____
11:30 _____	6:30 _____
12:00 _____	7:00 _____
12:30 _____	7:30 _____

Impact   Opportunity   Connection

Stay hydrated!

Step goal: _____   Steps completed: _____   Movement goal: _____

NOTES

To Do

Shopping List

Appointments to Make

Power Down

GRATITUDE

NAILED IT!

REFLECTION

_____
_____
_____
_____
_____
_____
_____
_____
_____
_____

AWARENESS

_____
_____
_____
_____

Commitments Completed

H:

H:

W:

Today's Wins

My HHW Score & Why

H: 1 2 3 4 5
_____
_____

H: 1 2 3 4 5
_____
_____

W: 1 2 3 4 5
_____
_____

Daily Total: _____

Power Up

AFFIRMATIONS

TODAY'S MANTRA

Date ___ / ___

SMTWTFS

TODAY'S THOUGHTS

_____
_____
_____
_____
_____
_____
_____
_____
_____
_____

BRIGHT IDEAS

_____
_____
_____
_____

3 Commitments	Habits	How I Will Lead
H:	Start:	Myself:
H:	Stop:	
W:	Continue:	Others:

The three A's of the Game: Awareness, Action & Accountability

TOP 3 PRIORITIES

1.

2.

3.

Power Play

Date ___ / ___
SMTWTFS

CALLS:

To make   To return

6:00 _____	1:00 _____
6:30 _____	1:30 _____
7:00 _____	2:00 _____
7:30 _____	2:30 _____
8:00 _____	3:00 _____
8:30 _____	3:30 _____
9:00 _____	4:00 _____
9:30 _____	4:30 _____
10:00 _____	5:00 _____
10:30 _____	5:30 _____
11:00 _____	6:00 _____
11:30 _____	6:30 _____
12:00 _____	7:00 _____
12:30 _____	7:30 _____

Impact

Opportunity

Connection

Stay hydrated!

Step goal: _____   Steps completed: _____   Movement goal: _____

NOTES

_____
_____
_____
_____
_____
_____
_____
_____
_____
_____
_____
_____
_____
_____
_____
_____
_____
_____
_____
_____
_____
_____

To Do	Shopping List	Appointments to Make

Power Down

GRATITUDE

NAILED IT!

REFLECTION

_____
_____
_____
_____
_____
_____
_____
_____
_____
_____

AWARENESS

_____
_____
_____
_____

Commitments Completed	Today's Wins	My HHW Score & Why
H:		H: 1 2 3 4 5
		_____
		_____
H:		H: 1 2 3 4 5
		_____
		_____
W:		W: 1 2 3 4 5
		_____
		_____
		Daily Total: _____

AFFIRMATIONS

Power Up

Date ___ / ___

SMTWTFS

TODAY'S MANTRA

TODAY'S THOUGHTS

_____
_____
_____
_____
_____
_____
_____
_____
_____
_____

BRIGHT IDEAS

_____
_____
_____
_____

3 Commitments	Habits	How I Will Lead
H:	Start:	Myself:
H:	Stop:	
W:	Continue:	Others:

Play full out, never burn out.

TOP 3 PRIORITIES

1.

2.

3.

Power Play

Date ___ / ___

SMTWTFS

CALLS:

To make   To return

6:00	1:00
6:30	1:30
7:00	2:00
7:30	2:30
8:00	3:00
8:30	3:30
9:00	4:00
9:30	4:30
10:00	5:00
10:30	5:30
11:00	6:00
11:30	6:30
12:00	7:00
12:30	7:30

Impact

Opportunity

Connection

Stay hydrated!

Step goal: _____   Steps completed: _____   Movement goal: _____

NOTES

_____

_____

_____

_____

_____

_____

_____

_____

_____

_____

_____

_____

_____

_____

_____

_____

_____

_____

_____

_____

_____

_____

To Do	Shopping List	Appointments to Make

Power Down

GRATITUDE

NAILED IT!

REFLECTION

_____
_____
_____
_____
_____
_____
_____
_____
_____
_____

AWARENESS

_____
_____
_____
_____

Commitments Completed	Today's Wins	My HHW Score & Why
H:		H: 1 2 3 4 5
		_____
		_____
H:		H: 1 2 3 4 5
		_____
		_____
W:		W: 1 2 3 4 5
		_____
		_____
		Daily Total: _____

AFFIRMATIONS

Power Up

Date ___ / ___

SMTWTFS

TODAY'S MANTRA

TODAY'S THOUGHTS

_____
_____
_____
_____
_____
_____
_____
_____
_____

BRIGHT IDEAS

_____
_____
_____
_____

3 Commitments	Habits	How I Will Lead
H:	Start:	Myself:
H:	Stop:	
W:	Continue:	Others:

How we do games is often how we do life.

TOP 3 PRIORITIES

1.

2.

3.

Power Play

Date ___ / ___
SMTWTFS

CALLS:
To make   To return

6:00	_____	1:00	_____
6:30	_____	1:30	_____
7:00	_____	2:00	_____
7:30	_____	2:30	_____
8:00	_____	3:00	_____
8:30	_____	3:30	_____
9:00	_____	4:00	_____
9:30	_____	4:30	_____
10:00	_____	5:00	_____
10:30	_____	5:30	_____
11:00	_____	6:00	_____
11:30	_____	6:30	_____
12:00	_____	7:00	_____
12:30	_____	7:30	_____

Impact   Opportunity   Connection

Stay hydrated!

Step goal: _____   Steps completed: _____   Movement goal: _____

NOTES

_____
_____
_____
_____
_____
_____
_____
_____
_____
_____
_____
_____
_____
_____
_____
_____
_____
_____
_____
_____
_____
_____

To Do

Shopping List

Appointments to Make

Power Down

GRATITUDE

NAILED IT!

REFLECTION

_____

_____

_____

_____

_____

_____

_____

_____

_____

_____

AWARENESS

_____

_____

_____

_____

Commitments Completed

H:

H:

W:

Today's Wins

My HHW Score & Why

H: 1 2 3 4 5

_____

_____

H: 1 2 3 4 5

_____

_____

W: 1 2 3 4 5

_____

_____

Daily Total: _____

Power Up

TODAY'S THOUGHTS

_____
_____
_____
_____
_____
_____
_____
_____
_____
_____

BRIGHT IDEAS

_____
_____
_____
_____

3 Commitments	Habits	How I Will Lead
H:	Start:	Myself:
H:	Stop:	
W:	Continue:	Others:

"A winner is a dreamer who never gives up."
~ Nelson Mandela

TOP 3 PRIORITIES

Power Play

Date ___ / ___
SMTWTFS

CALLS:
To make   To return

1.

2.

3.

6:00	_____	1:00	_____
6:30	_____	1:30	_____
7:00	_____	2:00	_____
7:30	_____	2:30	_____
8:00	_____	3:00	_____
8:30	_____	3:30	_____
9:00	_____	4:00	_____
9:30	_____	4:30	_____
10:00	_____	5:00	_____
10:30	_____	5:30	_____
11:00	_____	6:00	_____
11:30	_____	6:30	_____
12:00	_____	7:00	_____
12:30	_____	7:30	_____

Impact   Opportunity   Connection

Stay hydrated!
Step goal: _____   Steps completed: _____   Movement goal: _____

NOTES

_____

_____

_____

_____

_____

_____

_____

_____

_____

_____

_____

_____

_____

_____

_____

_____

_____

_____

_____

_____

_____

To Do	Shopping List	Appointments to Make

Power Down

GRATITUDE

NAILED IT!

REFLECTION

_____
_____
_____
_____
_____
_____
_____
_____
_____
_____

AWARENESS

_____
_____
_____
_____

Commitments Completed	Today's Wins	My HHW Score & Why
H:		H: 1 2 3 4 5
		_____
		_____
H:		H: 1 2 3 4 5
		_____
		_____
W:		W: 1 2 3 4 5
		_____
		_____
		Daily Total: _____

AFFIRMATIONS

Power Up

Date ___ / ___
SMTWTFS

TODAY'S MANTRA

TODAY'S THOUGHTS

_____
_____
_____
_____
_____
_____
_____
_____
_____
_____

BRIGHT IDEAS

_____
_____
_____
_____

3 Commitments

H:

H:

W:

Habits

Start:

Stop:

Continue:

How I Will Lead

Myself:

Others:

"Let's Rock This!"
~ Gina Pigott

TOP 3 PRIORITIES

Power Play

CALLS:
To make   To return

1.

2.

3.

Date ___ / ___
SMTWTFS

6:00 _____	1:00 _____
6:30 _____	1:30 _____
7:00 _____	2:00 _____
7:30 _____	2:30 _____
8:00 _____	3:00 _____
8:30 _____	3:30 _____
9:00 _____	4:00 _____
9:30 _____	4:30 _____
10:00 _____	5:00 _____
10:30 _____	5:30 _____
11:00 _____	6:00 _____
11:30 _____	6:30 _____
12:00 _____	7:00 _____
12:30 _____	7:30 _____

Impact   Opportunity   Connection

Stay hydrated!

Step goal: _____   Steps completed: _____   Movement goal: _____

NOTES

To Do

Shopping List

Appointments to Make

Power Down

GRATITUDE

NAILED IT!

REFLECTION

_____
_____
_____
_____
_____
_____
_____
_____
_____

AWARENESS

_____
_____
_____
_____

Commitments Completed

H:

H:

W:

Today's Wins

My HHW Score & Why

H: 1 2 3 4 5
_____
_____

H: 1 2 3 4 5
_____
_____

W: 1 2 3 4 5
_____
_____

Daily Total: _____

02 GOAL SETTING & ACHIEVING

"Goals must INSPIRE you
or they will EXPIRE you!"

~ Jim Bunch

week two

week two
GOAL SETTING & ACHIEVING

GOALS

GOAL SETTING & ACHIEVING

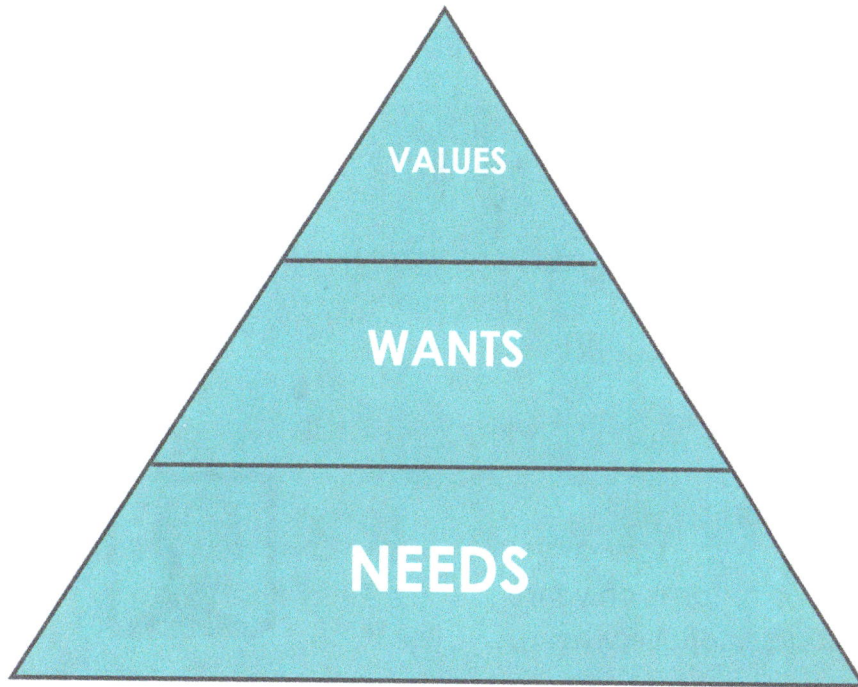

VALUES

WANTS

NEEDS

Needs based goals are things like time, space, money, love, information, food, exercise, etc... They are things you must have to be at your best. Without your needs being met, life often becomes difficult and stressful. When you satisfy a need, there is a sense of satisfaction or relief.

Wants are things that appeal to you and you want to acquire or experience such as a vacation, promotion, gourmet meal, sex, new car, etc. You usually feel a sense of gratification when you get something you want. Keep in mind the gratifying feeling of a want often fades within a short time after acquiring your want.

Values are something you naturally gravitate towards without prompting of a need or want. We will go in depth on your top 5 core values and how to orient your life around your values in an upcoming webinar.

Achieving goals is the part of the process where actions are required to reach your outcome. You must maintain the ability to focus on your desired goal, take daily actions and design environments to support the attainment of your goals.

02 GOALS

WHAT IS G.P.A.?

A **<u>Goal</u>** is a measurable outcome: a destination, a change in behavior or a tangible result within a timeline. Ex: To reach my ideal body weight of 135 lbs by March 15th.

A **<u>Project</u>** is one or more actions leading to a goal. Ex: To research and join a new gym, hire a trainer and craft a healthy eating plan.

An **<u>Action</u>** is a task or a physical test leading to the completion of a project or a goal. Any action having more than one step is usually a project. Ex: Go to the gym. Call your Accountability Partner and check in.

<u>Mind Dump Exercise</u>

This exercise will help you to clear your head and allow you to focus on your game, freeing yourself of overwhelm.

Think of a computer; if it has too many programs running it slows down and eventually crashes. Your mind is the same ... when it has too many things swirling around inside, it slows down and drains you, keeping you from focusing. Do this exercise any time you feel overwhelmed.

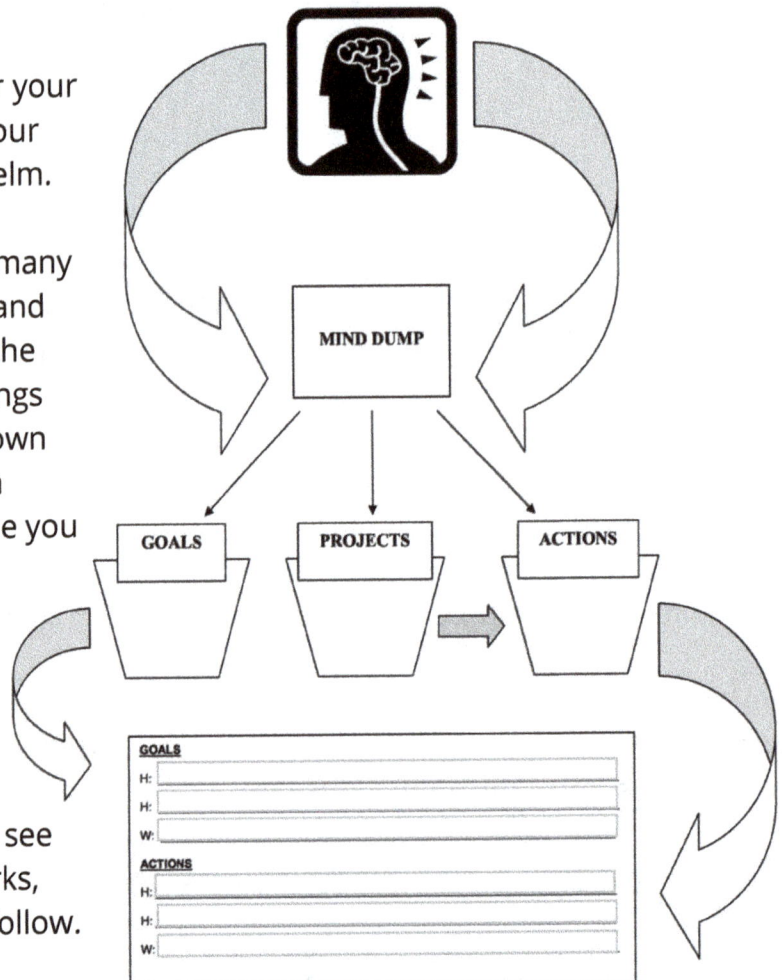

Refer to the following diagram to see how the Mind Dump process works, then begin with the 2 steps that follow.

MIND DUMP

GOALS   PROJECTS   ACTIONS

GOALS
H:
H:
W:

ACTIONS
H:
H:
W:

MIND DUMP

Step 1 - Clear your head by using the mind dump to get everything out of your head onto paper (this could be tolerations, things you have to do, dreams, intentions, etc.) By doing this, it allows space to show up (like rebooting your computer) and allows you to prioritize and get clear on your goals, actions, and projects. You may notice a theme showing up around the items on your list, like one area of your life needs more attention than others.

WHAT'S YOUR GPA

Step 2 is to separate them into GOALS, PROJECTS, and ACTIONS based on the definitions from this lesson. From this you can then decide what to hold on to in the Game and what to let go of.

GOALS	PROJECTS	ACTIONS

Prioritize Your GPA

Step 3 is to put your Goals, Projects and Actions into order of importance then start taking action toward your GPA's.

GOALS	PROJECTS	ACTIONS

Scorecard / Habit Tracker

Happy Goal _____

Healthy Goal _____

Wealthy Goal _____

ultimate life

Week starting _____ Accountability Partner Name/# _____

DAILY ACTIONS

Happy Habits / Actions	Mon	Tues	Wed	Thurs	Fri

Healthy Habits / Actions	Mon	Tues	Wed	Thurs	Fri

Wealthy Habits / Actions	Mon	Tues	Wed	Thurs	Fri

⚙ Committed Habit   ☺ Completed Habit   ☒ Incomplete Habit   ✔ Bonus Habit

WEEKLY TOTAL | 0

AFFIRMATIONS

Power Up

Date ___ / ___
SMTWTFS

TODAY'S MANTRA

TODAY'S THOUGHTS

_____
_____
_____
_____
_____
_____
_____
_____
_____

BRIGHT IDEAS

_____
_____
_____
_____

3 Commitments	Habits	How I Will Lead
H:	Start:	Myself:
H:	Stop:	
		Others:
W:	Continue:	

"A goal without a timeline is just a dream."
~ Robert Herjavec

TOP 3 PRIORITIES

1.

2.

3.

Power Play

Date ___ / ___
SMTWTFS

6:00	1:00
6:30	1:30
7:00	2:00
7:30	2:30
8:00	3:00
8:30	3:30
9:00	4:00
9:30	4:30
10:00	5:00
10:30	5:30
11:00	6:00
11:30	6:30
12:00	7:00
12:30	7:30

Impact

Opportunity

Connection

Stay hydrated!

Step goal: _____   Steps completed: _____   Movement goal: _____

NOTES

To Do

Shopping List

Appointments to Make

Power Down

GRATITUDE

NAILED IT!

REFLECTION

_____
_____
_____
_____
_____
_____
_____
_____
_____
_____

AWARENESS

_____
_____
_____
_____

Commitments Completed	Today's Wins	My HHW Score & Why
H:		H: 1 2 3 4 5
		_____
		_____
H:		H: 1 2 3 4 5
		_____
		_____
W:		W: 1 2 3 4 5
		_____
		_____
		Daily Total: _____

AFFIRMATIONS

Power Up

Date ___ / ___
SMTWTFS

TODAY'S MANTRA

TODAY'S THOUGHTS

_____
_____
_____
_____
_____
_____
_____
_____
_____
_____

BRIGHT IDEAS

_____
_____
_____
_____

3 Commitments

H:

H:

W:

Habits

Start:

Stop:

Continue:

How I Will Lead

Myself:

Others:

Life is not static, it is dynamic and organic.

TOP 3 PRIORITIES

1.

2.

3.

Power Play

Date ___ / ___
SMTWTFS

CALLS:

To make   To return

6:00	_____	1:00	_____
6:30	_____	1:30	_____
7:00	_____	2:00	_____
7:30	_____	2:30	_____
8:00	_____	3:00	_____
8:30	_____	3:30	_____
9:00	_____	4:00	_____
9:30	_____	4:30	_____
10:00	_____	5:00	_____
10:30	_____	5:30	_____
11:00	_____	6:00	_____
11:30	_____	6:30	_____
12:00	_____	7:00	_____
12:30	_____	7:30	_____

Impact

Opportunity

Connection

Stay hydrated!

Step goal: _____   Steps completed: _____   Movement goal: _____

NOTES

_____
_____
_____
_____
_____
_____
_____
_____
_____
_____
_____
_____
_____
_____
_____
_____
_____
_____
_____
_____
_____
_____

To Do	Shopping List	Appointments to Make

Power Down

GRATITUDE

NAILED IT!

REFLECTION

_____
_____
_____
_____
_____
_____
_____
_____
_____
_____

AWARENESS

_____
_____
_____
_____

Commitments Completed

H:

H:

W:

Today's Wins

My HHW Score & Why

H: 1 2 3 4 5
_____
_____

H: 1 2 3 4 5
_____
_____

W: 1 2 3 4 5
_____
_____

Daily Total: _____

AFFIRMATIONS

Power Up

Date ___ / ___
SMTWTFS

TODAY'S MANTRA

TODAY'S THOUGHTS

_____
_____
_____
_____
_____
_____
_____
_____
_____

BRIGHT IDEAS

_____
_____
_____
_____

3 Commitments	Habits	How I Will Lead
H:	Start:	Myself:
H:	Stop:	
W:	Continue:	Others:

"Always be a Goal Digger."
~ Gina Pigott

TOP 3 PRIORITIES

Power Play

CALLS:

To make   To return

1.

2.

3.

Date ___ / ___
SMTWTFS

6:00		1:00
6:30		1:30
7:00		2:00
7:30		2:30
8:00		3:00
8:30		3:30
9:00		4:00
9:30		4:30
10:00		5:00
10:30		5:30
11:00		6:00
11:30		6:30
12:00		7:00
12:30		7:30

Impact   Opportunity   Connection

Stay hydrated!

Step goal: _____   Steps completed: _____   Movement goal: _____

NOTES

_____

_____

_____

_____

_____

_____

_____

_____

_____

_____

_____

_____

_____

_____

_____

_____

_____

_____

_____

_____

To Do	Shopping List	Appointments to Make

Power Down

GRATITUDE

NAILED IT!

REFLECTION

_____
_____
_____
_____
_____
_____
_____
_____
_____
_____

AWARENESS

_____
_____
_____
_____

Commitments Completed

H:

H:

W:

Today's Wins

My HHW Score & Why

H: 1 2 3 4 5
_____
_____

H: 1 2 3 4 5
_____
_____

W: 1 2 3 4 5
_____
_____

Daily Total: _____

AFFIRMATIONS

Power Up

Date ___ / ___
SMTWTFS

TODAY'S MANTRA

TODAY'S THOUGHTS

_____
_____
_____
_____
_____
_____
_____
_____
_____
_____

BRIGHT IDEAS

_____
_____
_____
_____

3 Commitments	Habits	How I Will Lead
H:	Start:	Myself:
H:	Stop:	
		Others:
W:	Continue:	

"Dreams don't work unless you do."
~ John C. Maxwell

TOP 3 PRIORITIES

Power Play

CALLS:
To make   To return

1.

2.

3.

Date ___ / ___
SMTWTFS

6:00 _____	1:00 _____
6:30 _____	1:30 _____
7:00 _____	2:00 _____
7:30 _____	2:30 _____
8:00 _____	3:00 _____
8:30 _____	3:30 _____
9:00 _____	4:00 _____
9:30 _____	4:30 _____
10:00 _____	5:00 _____
10:30 _____	5:30 _____
11:00 _____	6:00 _____
11:30 _____	6:30 _____
12:00 _____	7:00 _____
12:30 _____	7:30 _____

Impact   Opportunity   Connection

Stay hydrated!

Step goal: _____   Steps completed: _____   Movement goal: _____

NOTES

_____
_____
_____
_____
_____
_____
_____
_____
_____
_____
_____
_____
_____
_____
_____
_____
_____
_____
_____
_____
_____
_____

To Do	Shopping List	Appointments to Make

Power Down

GRATITUDE

NAILED IT!

REFLECTION

_____
_____
_____
_____
_____
_____
_____
_____
_____
_____

AWARENESS

_____
_____
_____
_____

Commitments Completed

H:

H:

W:

Today's Wins

My HHW Score & Why

H: 1 2 3 4 5
_____
_____

H: 1 2 3 4 5
_____
_____

W: 1 2 3 4 5
_____
_____

Daily Total: _____

AFFIRMATIONS

Power Up

Date ___ / ___
SMTWTFS

TODAY'S MANTRA

TODAY'S THOUGHTS

_____
_____
_____
_____
_____
_____
_____
_____
_____

BRIGHT IDEAS

_____
_____
_____
_____

3 Commitments	Habits	How I Will Lead
H:	Start:	Myself:
H:	Stop:	
W:	Continue:	Others:

"I've always believed that if you put in the work, the results will come."
~ Michael Jordan

TOP 3 PRIORITIES

Power Play

CALLS:

To make   To return

1.

2.

3.

Date ___ / ___
SMTWTFS

6:00		1:00
6:30		1:30
7:00		2:00
7:30		2:30
8:00		3:00
8:30		3:30
9:00		4:00
9:30		4:30
10:00		5:00
10:30		5:30
11:00		6:00
11:30		6:30
12:00		7:00
12:30		7:30

Impact   Opportunity   Connection

Stay hydrated!

Step goal: _____   Steps completed: _____   Movement goal: _____

NOTES

To Do

Shopping List

Appointments to Make

Power Down

GRATITUDE

NAILED IT!

REFLECTION

_____
_____
_____
_____
_____
_____
_____
_____
_____
_____

AWARENESS

_____
_____
_____
_____

Commitments Completed	Today's Wins	My HHW Score & Why
H:		H: 1 2 3 4 5
		_____
		_____
H:		H: 1 2 3 4 5
		_____
		_____
W:		W: 1 2 3 4 5
		_____
		_____
		Daily Total: _____

Power Up

AFFIRMATIONS

Date ___ / ___
SMTWTFS

TODAY'S MANTRA

TODAY'S THOUGHTS

_____
_____
_____
_____
_____
_____
_____
_____
_____
_____

BRIGHT IDEAS

_____
_____
_____
_____

3 Commitments	Habits	How I Will Lead
H:	Start:	Myself:
H:	Stop:	
W:	Continue:	Others:

"A goal should scare you a little and excite you a lot."
~ Joe Vitale

TOP 3 PRIORITIES

Power Play

CALLS:
To make   To return

1.

2.

3.

Date ___ / ___
SMTWTFS

6:00 _____	1:00 _____
6:30 _____	1:30 _____
7:00 _____	2:00 _____
7:30 _____	2:30 _____
8:00 _____	3:00 _____
8:30 _____	3:30 _____
9:00 _____	4:00 _____
9:30 _____	4:30 _____
10:00 _____	5:00 _____
10:30 _____	5:30 _____
11:00 _____	6:00 _____
11:30 _____	6:30 _____
12:00 _____	7:00 _____
12:30 _____	7:30 _____

Impact   Opportunity   Connection

Stay hydrated!

Step goal: _____   Steps completed: _____   Movement goal: _____

NOTES

_____

_____

_____

_____

_____

_____

_____

_____

_____

_____

_____

_____

_____

_____

_____

_____

_____

_____

_____

To Do	Shopping List	Appointments to Make

Power Down

GRATITUDE

NAILED IT!

REFLECTION

_____
_____
_____
_____
_____
_____
_____
_____
_____
_____

AWARENESS

_____
_____
_____
_____

Commitments Completed

H:

H:

W:

Today's Wins

My HHW Score & Why

H: 1 2 3 4 5

_____
_____

H: 1 2 3 4 5

_____
_____

W: 1 2 3 4 5

_____
_____

Daily Total: _____

AFFIRMATIONS

Power Up

Date ___ / ___
SMTWTFS

TODAY'S MANTRA

TODAY'S THOUGHTS

_____
_____
_____
_____
_____
_____
_____
_____
_____

BRIGHT IDEAS

_____
_____
_____
_____

3 Commitments	Habits	How I Will Lead
H:	Start:	Myself:
H:	Stop:	
W:	Continue:	Others:

Dream Big... Set Goals ... Take Actions.

TOP 3 PRIORITIES

Power Play

CALLS:

To make   To return

1.

2.

3.

Date ___ / ___

SMTWTFS

6:00	1:00
6:30	1:30
7:00	2:00
7:30	2:30
8:00	3:00
8:30	3:30
9:00	4:00
9:30	4:30
10:00	5:00
10:30	5:30
11:00	6:00
11:30	6:30
12:00	7:00
12:30	7:30

Impact

Opportunity

Connection

Stay hydrated!

Step goal: _____   Steps completed: _____   Movement goal: _____

NOTES

_____
_____
_____
_____
_____
_____
_____
_____
_____
_____
_____
_____
_____
_____
_____
_____
_____
_____
_____
_____
_____
_____

To Do	Shopping List	Appointments to Make

Power Down

GRATITUDE

NAILED IT!

REFLECTION

_____
_____
_____
_____
_____
_____
_____
_____
_____
_____

AWARENESS

_____
_____
_____
_____

Commitments Completed	Today's Wins	My HHW Score & Why
H:		H: 1 2 3 4 5
		_____
		_____
H:		H: 1 2 3 4 5
		_____
		_____
W:		W: 1 2 3 4 5
		_____
		_____
		Daily Total: _____

03 SIMPLIFY YOUR LIFE... THE POWER OF ELIMINATION

"To attain knowledge, add things every day. To attain wisdom, remove things every day."

~ Lao Tzu

week three

week three

SIMPLIFY YOUR LIFE... THE POWER OF ELIMINATION

ELIMINATING 03

What are some of the benefits of simplifying your life and eliminating clutter?

Focus

Free time to do what you love

Able to design your life as you choose

Increased energy

Peace of mind

Ability to stay present in the moment

Creates a feeling of lightness

More Happiness, Health and Wealth

_____

_____

_____

_____

_____

_____

Scorecard / Habit Tracker

Happy Goal _____

Healthy Goal _____

Wealthy Goal _____

ultimate life

Week starting _____ Accountability Partner Name/# _____

DAILY ACTIONS

Happy Habits / Actions	Mon	Tues	Wed	Thurs	Fri
_____					
_____					
_____					
_____					
_____					
_____					
_____					
_____					

Healthy Habits / Actions	Mon	Tues	Wed	Thurs	Fri
_____					
_____					
_____					
_____					
_____					
_____					
_____					
_____					

Wealthy Habits / Actions	Mon	Tues	Wed	Thurs	Fri
_____					
_____					
_____					
_____					
_____					
_____					
_____					
_____					

⚙ Committed Habit   ☺ Completed Habit   ☒ Incomplete Habit   ☑ Bonus Habit

WEEKLY TOTAL | 0

Power Up

AFFIRMATIONS

TODAY'S MANTRA

Date ___ / ___

SMTWTFS

TODAY'S THOUGHTS

_____
_____
_____
_____
_____
_____
_____
_____
_____
_____

BRIGHT IDEAS

_____
_____
_____
_____

3 Commitments	Habits	How I Will Lead
H:	Start:	Myself:
H:	Stop:	
		Others:
W:	Continue:	

"Clutter is not just the stuff on your floor - it's anything
that stands between you and the life you want to be living."
~ Peter Walsh

TOP 3 PRIORITIES

1.

2.

3.

Power Play

Date ___ / ___

SMTWTFS

CALLS:

To make   To return

6:00	1:00
6:30	1:30
7:00	2:00
7:30	2:30
8:00	3:00
8:30	3:30
9:00	4:00
9:30	4:30
10:00	5:00
10:30	5:30
11:00	6:00
11:30	6:30
12:00	7:00
12:30	7:30

Impact   Opportunity   Connection

Stay hydrated!

Step goal: _____   Steps completed: _____   Movement goal: _____

NOTES

_____
_____
_____
_____
_____
_____
_____
_____
_____
_____
_____
_____
_____
_____
_____
_____
_____
_____
_____
_____
_____
_____

To Do	Shopping List	Appointments to Make

Power Down

GRATITUDE

NAILED IT!

REFLECTION

_____
_____
_____
_____
_____
_____
_____
_____
_____
_____

AWARENESS

_____
_____
_____
_____

Commitments Completed	Today's Wins	My HHW Score & Why
H:		H: 1 2 3 4 5
		_____
		_____
H:		H: 1 2 3 4 5
		_____
		_____
W:		W: 1 2 3 4 5
		_____
		_____
		Daily Total: _____

AFFIRMATIONS

Power Up

Date ___ / ___

SMTWTFS

TODAY'S MANTRA

TODAY'S THOUGHTS

_____
_____
_____
_____
_____
_____
_____
_____
_____
_____

BRIGHT IDEAS

_____
_____
_____
_____
_____

3 Commitments	Habits	How I Will Lead
H:	Start:	Myself:
H:	Stop:	
		Others:
W:	Continue:	

Elimination requires courage and energy.

TOP 3 PRIORITIES

Power Play

CALLS:
To make   To return

1.

2.

3.

Date ___ / ___
SMTWTFS

Time		Time	
6:00		1:00	
6:30		1:30	
7:00		2:00	
7:30		2:30	
8:00		3:00	
8:30		3:30	
9:00		4:00	
9:30		4:30	
10:00		5:00	
10:30		5:30	
11:00		6:00	
11:30		6:30	
12:00		7:00	
12:30		7:30	

Impact   Opportunity   Connection

Stay hydrated!

Step goal: _____   Steps completed: _____   Movement goal: _____

NOTES

_____
_____
_____
_____
_____
_____
_____
_____
_____
_____
_____
_____
_____
_____
_____
_____
_____
_____
_____
_____
_____
_____

To Do	Shopping List	Appointments to Make

Power Down

GRATITUDE

NAILED IT!

REFLECTION

_____
_____
_____
_____
_____
_____
_____
_____
_____
_____

AWARENESS

_____
_____
_____
_____

Commitments Completed

H:

H:

W:

Today's Wins

My HHW Score & Why

H: 1 2 3 4 5
_____
_____

H: 1 2 3 4 5
_____
_____

W: 1 2 3 4 5
_____
_____

Daily Total: _____

AFFIRMATIONS

Power Up

Date ___ / ___
SMTWTFS

TODAY'S MANTRA

TODAY'S THOUGHTS

_____
_____
_____
_____
_____
_____
_____
_____
_____
_____

BRIGHT IDEAS

_____
_____
_____
_____

3 Commitments	Habits	How I Will Lead
H:	Start:	Myself:
H:	Stop:	
W:	Continue:	Others:

"In life you get what you tolerate."
~ Mike Ditka

TOP 3 PRIORITIES

1.

2.

3.

Power Play

Date ___ / ___
SMTWTFS

CALLS:

To make   To return

Time		Time	
6:00		1:00	
6:30		1:30	
7:00		2:00	
7:30		2:30	
8:00		3:00	
8:30		3:30	
9:00		4:00	
9:30		4:30	
10:00		5:00	
10:30		5:30	
11:00		6:00	
11:30		6:30	
12:00		7:00	
12:30		7:30	

Impact

Opportunity

Connection

Stay hydrated!

Step goal: _____   Steps completed: _____   Movement goal: _____

NOTES

To Do

Shopping List

Appointments to Make

Power Down

GRATITUDE

NAILED IT!

REFLECTION

_____
_____
_____
_____
_____
_____
_____
_____
_____
_____

AWARENESS

_____
_____
_____
_____

Commitments Completed	Today's Wins	My HHW Score & Why
H: H: W:		H: 1 2 3 4 5 _____ _____ H: 1 2 3 4 5 _____ _____ W: 1 2 3 4 5 _____ _____ Daily Total: _____

AFFIRMATIONS

Power Up

Date ___ / ___

SMTWTFS

TODAY'S MANTRA

TODAY'S THOUGHTS

_____
_____
_____
_____
_____
_____
_____
_____
_____
_____

BRIGHT IDEAS

_____
_____
_____
_____

3 Commitments	Habits	How I Will Lead
H:	Start:	Myself:
H:	Stop:	
W:	Continue:	Others:

"Your home is a living space, not a storage space."
~ Francine Jay

TOP 3 PRIORITIES

Power Play

To make   To return

1.

2.

3.

Date ___ / ___
SMTWTFS

6:00	1:00
6:30	1:30
7:00	2:00
7:30	2:30
8:00	3:00
8:30	3:30
9:00	4:00
9:30	4:30
10:00	5:00
10:30	5:30
11:00	6:00
11:30	6:30
12:00	7:00
12:30	7:30

Impact   Opportunity   Connection

Stay hydrated!

Step goal: _____   Steps completed: _____   Movement goal: _____

NOTES

_____
_____
_____
_____
_____
_____
_____
_____
_____
_____
_____
_____
_____
_____
_____
_____
_____
_____
_____
_____
_____
_____

To Do	Shopping List	Appointments to Make

Power Down

GRATITUDE

NAILED IT!

REFLECTION

_____
_____
_____
_____
_____
_____
_____
_____
_____

AWARENESS

_____
_____
_____
_____

Commitments Completed

H:

H:

W:

Today's Wins

My HHW Score & Why

H: 1 2 3 4 5
_____
_____

H: 1 2 3 4 5
_____
_____

W: 1 2 3 4 5
_____
_____

Daily Total: _____

AFFIRMATIONS

Power Up

Date ___ / ___
SMTWTFS

TODAY'S MANTRA

TODAY'S THOUGHTS

_____
_____
_____
_____
_____
_____
_____
_____
_____
_____

BRIGHT IDEAS

_____
_____
_____
_____

3 Commitments	Habits	How I Will Lead
H:	Start:	Myself:
H:	Stop:	
W:	Continue:	Others:

"Simplicity succeeds. Complexity kills."
~ Jim Bunch

TOP 3 PRIORITIES

1.

2.

3.

Power Play

Date ___ / ___

SMTWTFS

CALLS:

To make   To return

6:00		1:00	
6:30		1:30	
7:00		2:00	
7:30		2:30	
8:00		3:00	
8:30		3:30	
9:00		4:00	
9:30		4:30	
10:00		5:00	
10:30		5:30	
11:00		6:00	
11:30		6:30	
12:00		7:00	
12:30		7:30	

Impact

Opportunity

Connection

Stay hydrated!

Step goal: _____   Steps completed: _____   Movement goal: _____

NOTES

To Do

Shopping List

Appointments to Make

Power Down

GRATITUDE

NAILED IT!

REFLECTION

_____
_____
_____
_____
_____
_____
_____
_____
_____
_____

AWARENESS

_____
_____
_____
_____

Commitments Completed	Today's Wins	My HHW Score & Why
H:		H: 1 2 3 4 5
		_____
		_____
H:		H: 1 2 3 4 5
		_____
		_____
W:		W: 1 2 3 4 5
		_____
		_____
		Daily Total: _____

AFFIRMATIONS

Power Up

Date ___ / ___
SMTWTFS

TODAY'S MANTRA

TODAY'S THOUGHTS

_____
_____
_____
_____
_____
_____
_____
_____
_____

BRIGHT IDEAS

_____
_____
_____
_____

3 Commitments

H:

H:

W:

Habits

Start:

Stop:

Continue:

How I Will Lead

Myself:

Others:

Progress over Perfection.

TOP 3 PRIORITIES

Power Play

CALLS:

To make   To return

1.

2.

3.

Date ___ / ___
SMTWTFS

6:00	1:00
6:30	1:30
7:00	2:00
7:30	2:30
8:00	3:00
8:30	3:30
9:00	4:00
9:30	4:30
10:00	5:00
10:30	5:30
11:00	6:00
11:30	6:30
12:00	7:00
12:30	7:30

Impact

Opportunity

Connection

Stay hydrated!

Step goal: _____   Steps completed: _____   Movement goal: _____

NOTES

_____

_____

_____

_____

_____

_____

_____

_____

_____

_____

_____

_____

_____

_____

_____

_____

_____

_____

_____

_____

To Do	Shopping List	Appointments to Make

Power Down

GRATITUDE

NAILED IT!

REFLECTION

_____
_____
_____
_____
_____
_____
_____
_____
_____
_____

AWARENESS

_____
_____
_____
_____

Commitments Completed

H:

H:

W:

Today's Wins

My HHW Score & Why

H: 1 2 3 4 5
_____
_____

H: 1 2 3 4 5
_____
_____

W: 1 2 3 4 5
_____
_____

Daily Total: _____

AFFIRMATIONS

Power Up

Date ___ / ___
SMTWTFS

TODAY'S MANTRA

TODAY'S THOUGHTS

_____
_____
_____
_____
_____
_____
_____
_____
_____
_____

BRIGHT IDEAS

_____
_____
_____
_____

3 Commitments	Habits	How I Will Lead
H:	Start:	Myself:
H:	Stop:	
		Others:
W:	Continue:	

"It's all about choices!"
~ Gina Pigott

TOP 3 PRIORITIES

Power Play

1.

2.

3.

Date ___ / ___
SMTWTFS

6:00	_____	1:00	_____
6:30	_____	1:30	_____
7:00	_____	2:00	_____
7:30	_____	2:30	_____
8:00	_____	3:00	_____
8:30	_____	3:30	_____
9:00	_____	4:00	_____
9:30	_____	4:30	_____
10:00	_____	5:00	_____
10:30	_____	5:30	_____
11:00	_____	6:00	_____
11:30	_____	6:30	_____
12:00	_____	7:00	_____
12:30	_____	7:30	_____

Impact

Opportunity

Connection

Stay hydrated!

Step goal: _____   Steps completed: _____   Movement goal: _____

NOTES

To Do

Shopping List

Appointments to Make

Power Down

GRATITUDE

NAILED IT!

REFLECTION

_____
_____
_____
_____
_____
_____
_____
_____
_____
_____

AWARENESS

_____
_____
_____
_____

Commitments Completed

H:

H:

W:

Today's Wins

My HHW Score & Why

H: 1 2 3 4 5
_____
_____

H: 1 2 3 4 5
_____
_____

W: 1 2 3 4 5
_____
_____

Daily Total: _____

04

WINNING THE INNER GAME: REPROGRAMMING YOUR MIND FOR SUCCESS

"You are not your mind; you may think you are your mind, but you are not."

~ Jim Bunch

week four

week four

WINNING THE INNER GAME: REPROGRAMMING YOUR MIND FOR SUCCESS

Our Belief Systems

Belief Systems are like filters that affect your view of the world. These beliefs can become your perception or reality.

There are many types of beliefs and they fall into 2 types of belief systems: **Empowering and Limiting**.

Empowering belief systems give you energy, confidence, make you feel good and get you to take action in a positive direction.

Dis-empowering beliefs drain your energy, make you feel bad and cause you not to want to take action or to take unhealthy actions.

Limiting Beliefs can be our FEARS, EXCUSES AND RATION-LIES.

Henry Ford once said, "If you think you can
or you think you can't,
you are right."

It does not matter whether you think you are right or wrong, or if your beliefs are true or false; what matters is "Do They Serve You and those around you for your best and highest good?"

The Stickman & The Results Model

All results we produce in life - our Happiness, Health, Wealth - are a reflection of our past programming and conditioning.

The simple explanation came from a chiropractor in Texas: "the stickman".

- Your Beliefs/Thoughts generate the perceptions you have in life.
- Your Perceptions generate the feelings you have.
- Your Feelings generate your motivation.
- Your Motivation leads to your actions.
- Your "Consistent" Actions determine your results.

_____

_____

_____

_____

_____

_____

_____

_____

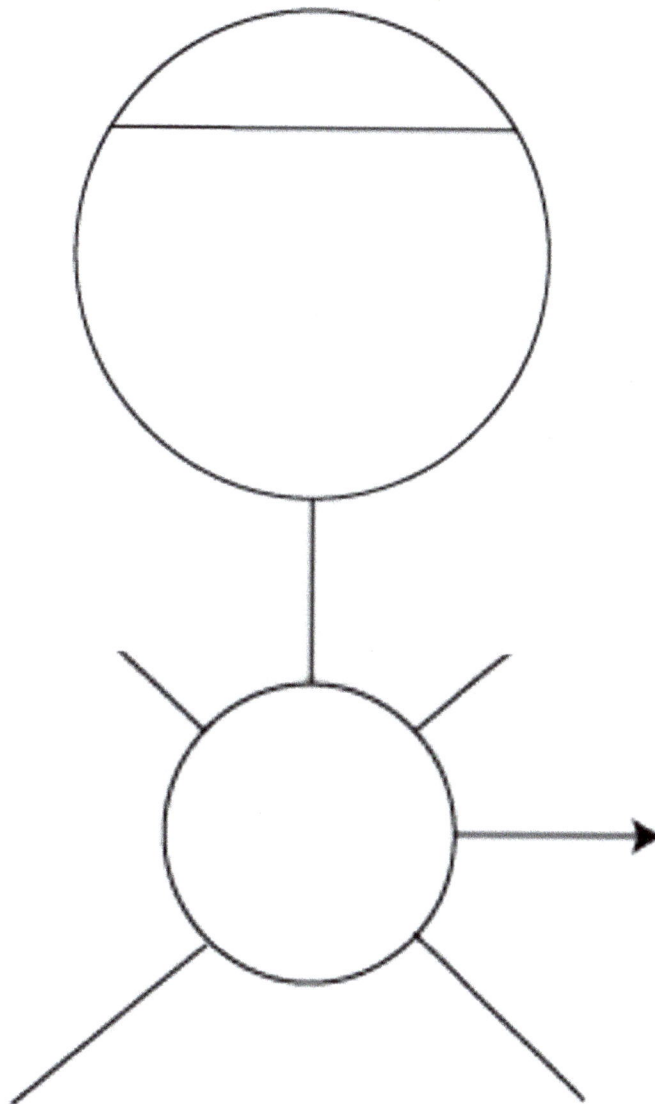

Scorecard / Habit Tracker

Happy Goal _____

Healthy Goal _____

Wealthy Goal _____

Week starting _____ Accountability Partner Name/# _____

ultimate life

DAILY ACTIONS

Happy Habits / Actions	Mon	Tues	Wed	Thurs	Fri
_____					
_____					
_____					
_____					
_____					
_____					
_____					

Healthy Habits / Actions	Mon	Tues	Wed	Thurs	Fri
_____					
_____					
_____					
_____					
_____					
_____					
_____					

Wealthy Habits / Actions	Mon	Tues	Wed	Thurs	Fri
_____					
_____					
_____					
_____					
_____					
_____					
_____					

⚙ Committed Habit   ☺ Completed Habit   ☒ Incomplete Habit   ☑ Bonus Habit

WEEKLY TOTAL | **0**

Power Up

AFFIRMATIONS

Date ___ / ___
SMTWTFS

TODAY'S MANTRA

TODAY'S THOUGHTS

_____
_____
_____
_____
_____
_____
_____
_____
_____
_____

BRIGHT IDEAS

_____
_____
_____
_____

3 Commitments	Habits	How I Will Lead
H:	Start:	Myself:
H:	Stop:	
W:	Continue:	Others:

"Nothing is impossible. The word itself says 'I'm Possible'."
~ Audrey Hepburn

TOP 3 PRIORITIES

1.

2.

3.

Power Play

Date ___ / ___
SMTWTFS

CALLS:
To make   To return

Time		Time	
6:00		1:00	
6:30		1:30	
7:00		2:00	
7:30		2:30	
8:00		3:00	
8:30		3:30	
9:00		4:00	
9:30		4:30	
10:00		5:00	
10:30		5:30	
11:00		6:00	
11:30		6:30	
12:00		7:00	
12:30		7:30	

Impact

Opportunity

Connection

Stay hydrated!

Step goal: _____   Steps completed: _____   Movement goal: _____

NOTES

_____

_____

_____

_____

_____

_____

_____

_____

_____

_____

_____

_____

_____

_____

_____

_____

_____

_____

_____

_____

To Do	Shopping List	Appointments to Make

Power Down

GRATITUDE

NAILED IT!

REFLECTION

_____
_____
_____
_____
_____
_____
_____
_____
_____
_____

AWARENESS

_____
_____
_____
_____

Commitments Completed	Today's Wins	My HHW Score & Why
H:		H: 1 2 3 4 5
		_____
		_____
H:		H: 1 2 3 4 5
		_____
		_____
W:		W: 1 2 3 4 5
		_____
		_____
		Daily Total: _____

Power Up

AFFIRMATIONS

TODAY'S MANTRA

Date ___ / ___
SMTWTFS

TODAY'S THOUGHTS

_____
_____
_____
_____
_____
_____
_____
_____
_____
_____

BRIGHT IDEAS

_____
_____
_____
_____

3 Commitments	Habits	How I Will Lead
H:	Start:	Myself:
H:	Stop:	
		Others:
W:	Continue:	

"All personal breakthroughs begin with a change in beliefs."
~ Tony Robbins

TOP 3 PRIORITIES

Power Play

CALLS:
To make   To return

1.

2.

3.

Date ___ / ___
SMTWTFS

6:00	1:00
6:30	1:30
7:00	2:00
7:30	2:30
8:00	3:00
8:30	3:30
9:00	4:00
9:30	4:30
10:00	5:00
10:30	5:30
11:00	6:00
11:30	6:30
12:00	7:00
12:30	7:30

Impact   Opportunity   Connection

Stay hydrated!

Step goal: _____   Steps completed: _____   Movement goal: _____

NOTES

_____
_____
_____
_____
_____
_____
_____
_____
_____
_____
_____
_____
_____
_____
_____
_____
_____
_____
_____
_____
_____

To Do	Shopping List	Appointments to Make

Power Down

GRATITUDE

NAILED IT!

REFLECTION

_____
_____
_____
_____
_____
_____
_____
_____
_____
_____

AWARENESS

_____
_____
_____
_____

Commitments Completed	Today's Wins	My HHW Score & Why
H:		H: 1 2 3 4 5
		_____
		_____
H:		H: 1 2 3 4 5
		_____
		_____
W:		W: 1 2 3 4 5
		_____
		_____
		Daily Total: _____

Power Up

AFFIRMATIONS

Date ___ / ___

SMTWTFS

TODAY'S MANTRA

TODAY'S THOUGHTS

_____
_____
_____
_____
_____
_____
_____
_____
_____
_____

BRIGHT IDEAS

_____
_____
_____
_____

3 Commitments	Habits	How I Will Lead
H:	Start:	Myself:
H:	Stop:	
		Others:
W:	Continue:	

"Believe you can and you're halfway there."
~ Theodore Roosevelt

TOP 3 PRIORITIES

1.

2.

3.

Power Play

Date ___ / ___

SMTWTFS

CALLS:

To make   To return

6:00 _____	1:00 _____
6:30 _____	1:30 _____
7:00 _____	2:00 _____
7:30 _____	2:30 _____
8:00 _____	3:00 _____
8:30 _____	3:30 _____
9:00 _____	4:00 _____
9:30 _____	4:30 _____
10:00 _____	5:00 _____
10:30 _____	5:30 _____
11:00 _____	6:00 _____
11:30 _____	6:30 _____
12:00 _____	7:00 _____
12:30 _____	7:30 _____

Impact   Opportunity   Connection

Stay hydrated!

Step goal: _____   Steps completed: _____   Movement goal: _____

NOTES

_____

_____

_____

_____

_____

_____

_____

_____

_____

_____

_____

_____

_____

_____

_____

_____

_____

_____

_____

_____

To Do	Shopping List	Appointments to Make

Power Down

GRATITUDE

NAILED IT!

REFLECTION

_____
_____
_____
_____
_____
_____
_____
_____
_____

AWARENESS

_____
_____
_____
_____

Commitments Completed

H:

H:

W:

Today's Wins

My HHW Score & Why

H: 1 2 3 4 5
_____
_____

H: 1 2 3 4 5
_____
_____

W: 1 2 3 4 5
_____
_____

Daily Total: _____

AFFIRMATIONS

Power Up

Date ___ / ___
SMTWTFS

TODAY'S MANTRA

TODAY'S THOUGHTS

_____
_____
_____
_____
_____
_____
_____
_____
_____
_____

BRIGHT IDEAS

_____
_____
_____
_____

3 Commitments	Habits	How I Will Lead
H:	Start:	Myself:
H:	Stop:	
		Others:
W:	Continue:	

"If my mind can conceive it, and my heart can believe it, then I can achieve it."
~ Muhammed Ali

TOP 3 PRIORITIES

1.

2.

3.

Power Play

Date ___ / ___

SMTWTFS

CALLS:

To make   To return

6:00	1:00
6:30	1:30
7:00	2:00
7:30	2:30
8:00	3:00
8:30	3:30
9:00	4:00
9:30	4:30
10:00	5:00
10:30	5:30
11:00	6:00
11:30	6:30
12:00	7:00
12:30	7:30

Impact   Opportunity   Connection

Stay hydrated!

Step goal: _____   Steps completed: _____   Movement goal: _____

NOTES

_____

_____

_____

_____

_____

_____

_____

_____

_____

_____

_____

_____

_____

_____

_____

_____

_____

_____

_____

_____

To Do	Shopping List	Appointments to Make

Power Down

GRATITUDE

NAILED IT!

REFLECTION

_____
_____
_____
_____
_____
_____
_____
_____
_____

AWARENESS

_____
_____
_____
_____

Commitments Completed

H:

H:

W:

Today's Wins

My HHW Score & Why

H: 1 2 3 4 5
_____
_____

H: 1 2 3 4 5
_____
_____

W: 1 2 3 4 5
_____
_____

Daily Total: _____

AFFIRMATIONS

Power Up

Date ___ / ___
SMTWTFS

TODAY'S MANTRA

TODAY'S THOUGHTS

_____
_____
_____
_____
_____
_____
_____
_____
_____
_____

BRIGHT IDEAS

_____
_____
_____
_____

3 Commitments

H:

H:

W:

Habits

Start:

Stop:

Continue:

How I Will Lead

Myself:

Others:

"If you change the way you look at things, the things you look at change."
~ Wayne Dyer

TOP 3 PRIORITIES

Power Play

CALLS:

To make   To return

1.

2.

3.

Date ___ / ___
SMTWTFS

6:00 _____	1:00 _____
6:30 _____	1:30 _____
7:00 _____	2:00 _____
7:30 _____	2:30 _____
8:00 _____	3:00 _____
8:30 _____	3:30 _____
9:00 _____	4:00 _____
9:30 _____	4:30 _____
10:00 _____	5:00 _____
10:30 _____	5:30 _____
11:00 _____	6:00 _____
11:30 _____	6:30 _____
12:00 _____	7:00 _____
12:30 _____	7:30 _____

Impact   Opportunity   Connection

Stay hydrated!

Step goal: _____   Steps completed: _____   Movement goal: _____

NOTES

_____
_____
_____
_____
_____
_____
_____
_____
_____
_____
_____
_____
_____
_____
_____
_____
_____
_____
_____
_____
_____
_____

To Do	Shopping List	Appointments to Make

Power Down

GRATITUDE

NAILED IT!

REFLECTION

_____
_____
_____
_____
_____
_____
_____
_____
_____
_____

AWARENESS

_____
_____
_____
_____

Commitments Completed

H:

H:

W:

Today's Wins

My HHW Score & Why

H: 1 2 3 4 5
_____
_____

H: 1 2 3 4 5
_____
_____

W: 1 2 3 4 5
_____
_____

Daily Total: _____

AFFIRMATIONS

Power Up

Date ___ / ___
SMTWTFS

TODAY'S MANTRA

TODAY'S THOUGHTS

_____
_____
_____
_____
_____
_____
_____
_____
_____
_____

BRIGHT IDEAS

_____
_____
_____
_____

3 Commitments	Habits	How I Will Lead
H:	Start:	Myself:
H:	Stop:	
		Others:
W:	Continue:	

Your brain is your hardware and your mind is your software.
You are not the program, you are the programmer.

TOP 3 PRIORITIES

Power Play

CALLS:
To make   To return

1.

2.

3.

Date ___ / ___
SMTWTFS

6:00	1:00
6:30	1:30
7:00	2:00
7:30	2:30
8:00	3:00
8:30	3:30
9:00	4:00
9:30	4:30
10:00	5:00
10:30	5:30
11:00	6:00
11:30	6:30
12:00	7:00
12:30	7:30

Impact

Opportunity

Connection

Stay hydrated!

Step goal: _____   Steps completed: _____   Movement goal: _____

NOTES

_____

_____

_____

_____

_____

_____

_____

_____

_____

_____

_____

_____

_____

_____

_____

_____

_____

_____

_____

_____

_____

_____

To Do	Shopping List	Appointments to Make

Power Down

GRATITUDE

NAILED IT!

REFLECTION

_____
_____
_____
_____
_____
_____
_____
_____
_____
_____

AWARENESS

_____
_____
_____
_____

Commitments Completed	Today's Wins	My HHW Score & Why
H:		H: 1 2 3 4 5
		_____
		_____
H:		H: 1 2 3 4 5
		_____
		_____
W:		W: 1 2 3 4 5
		_____
		_____
		Daily Total: _____

Power Up

AFFIRMATIONS

TODAY'S MANTRA

Date ___ / ___
SMTWTFS

TODAY'S THOUGHTS

_____
_____
_____
_____
_____
_____
_____
_____
_____
_____

BRIGHT IDEAS

_____
_____
_____
_____

3 Commitments	Habits	How I Will Lead
H:	Start:	Myself:
H:	Stop:	
		Others:
W:	Continue:	

"An unquestioned belief becomes a guaranteed reality."
~ Jim Bunch

TOP 3 PRIORITIES

1.

2.

3.

Power Play

Date ___ / ___
SMTWTFS

CALLS:
To make   To return

6:00	1:00
6:30	1:30
7:00	2:00
7:30	2:30
8:00	3:00
8:30	3:30
9:00	4:00
9:30	4:30
10:00	5:00
10:30	5:30
11:00	6:00
11:30	6:30
12:00	7:00
12:30	7:30

Impact   Opportunity   Connection

Stay hydrated!

Step goal: _____   Steps completed: _____   Movement goal: _____

NOTES

_____
_____
_____
_____
_____
_____
_____
_____
_____
_____
_____
_____
_____
_____
_____
_____
_____
_____
_____
_____
_____

To Do	Shopping List	Appointments to Make

Power Down

GRATITUDE

NAILED IT!

REFLECTION

_____
_____
_____
_____
_____
_____
_____
_____
_____
_____

AWARENESS

_____
_____
_____
_____

Commitments Completed

H:

H:

W:

Today's Wins

My HHW Score & Why

H: 1 2 3 4 5
_____
_____

H: 1 2 3 4 5
_____
_____

W: 1 2 3 4 5
_____
_____

Daily Total: _____

05

THE 9 ENVIRONMENTS OF YOU

"Most people spend their whole life frustrated
trying to use willpower to change who they are.
When what they really need to know is virtually
all their thinking and behavior is determined
by their 9 environments.
If you set up the right environment, you will literally be
pulled toward your goals. This is what I mean by
'Delegate your success to your environment'."
~ Thomas Leonard, Author of *The Portable Coach*

week five

week five

THE 9 ENVIRONMENTS OF YOU

05

A Snapshot of the Environments

The following is a description of the environments you are surrounded by 24/7:

You

- The core of you that is unchanging

Memetic

- Ideas, Opinions, Concepts, Thoughts, Beliefs, Paradigm, Styles, Usages
- Information/knowledge you receive — coaching calls, books, tapes, seminars, media, magazines, articles, TV, Internet, Radio
- Passed down from generation to generation; language patterns

Body

- Your physical body (hair, skin, nails, posture)
- Health
- Your primary energy source (adrenaline vs. inspiration/choice)
- Somatic (Observer of our own body)

Self

- Feelings
- Passions
- Values
- Skills and unique assets
- Heart Gifts
- Amount of space in your life

Spiritual

- Spirit/Connections to God/Divine/Higher Power
- Spiritual Practices (prayer, meditation)

Relationships

- Family, Friends, Colleagues, Neighbors, people you connect with daily
- Staff/Assistants
- Mentors/Coaches
- Pets

Network

- Customers/Vendors
- The Internet/Web
- 6 Degrees of Separation
- Communities you belong to: church, dojo, schools, children's sports teams, associations, charities, meetings, Mastermind groups

Financial

- Money, investments, stocks, bonds, insurance
- People who support your financial well being (CPA, Employer, Lawyer, Real Estate Attorney, Financial Advisor)
- Tools that support you in wealth (budget, Expense Tracker, P&L, Quicken, QuickBooks...)

THE 9 ENVIRONMENTS OF YOU

05

Physical

- Home, office/desk, clutter
- Technology/Tools (phones, pagers, computers…)
- Possessions (car, artwork, toys, boats, accessories)
- Gym & equipment
- Sounds

Nature

- Life
- The Outdoors-parks, outdoor sporting events, camping, animals, zoo
- Geography (Southern CA vs.Northeast)
- Seasons - each has a different energy and influence on us

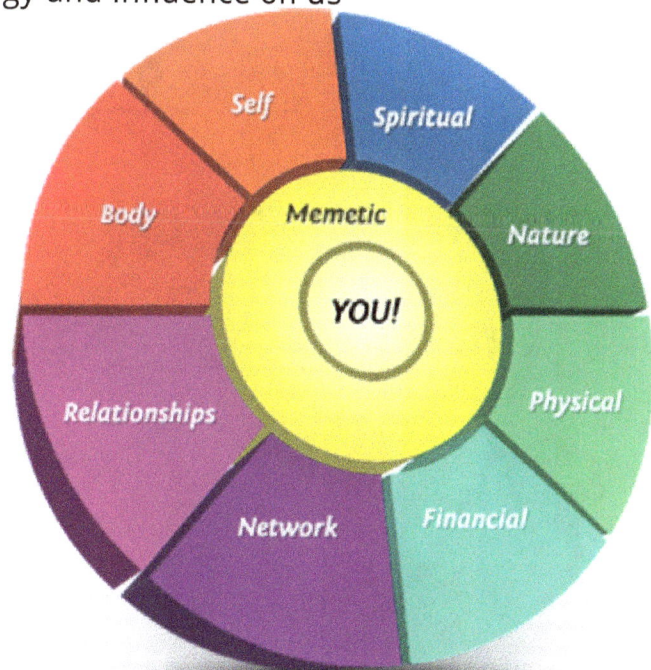

Self
Spiritual
Body
Memetic
Nature
YOU!
Relationships
Physical
Network
Financial

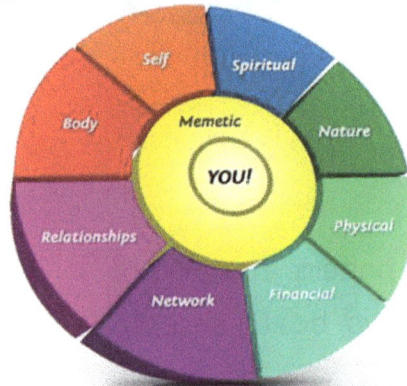

Everything is an Environment.

Environments are all connected.

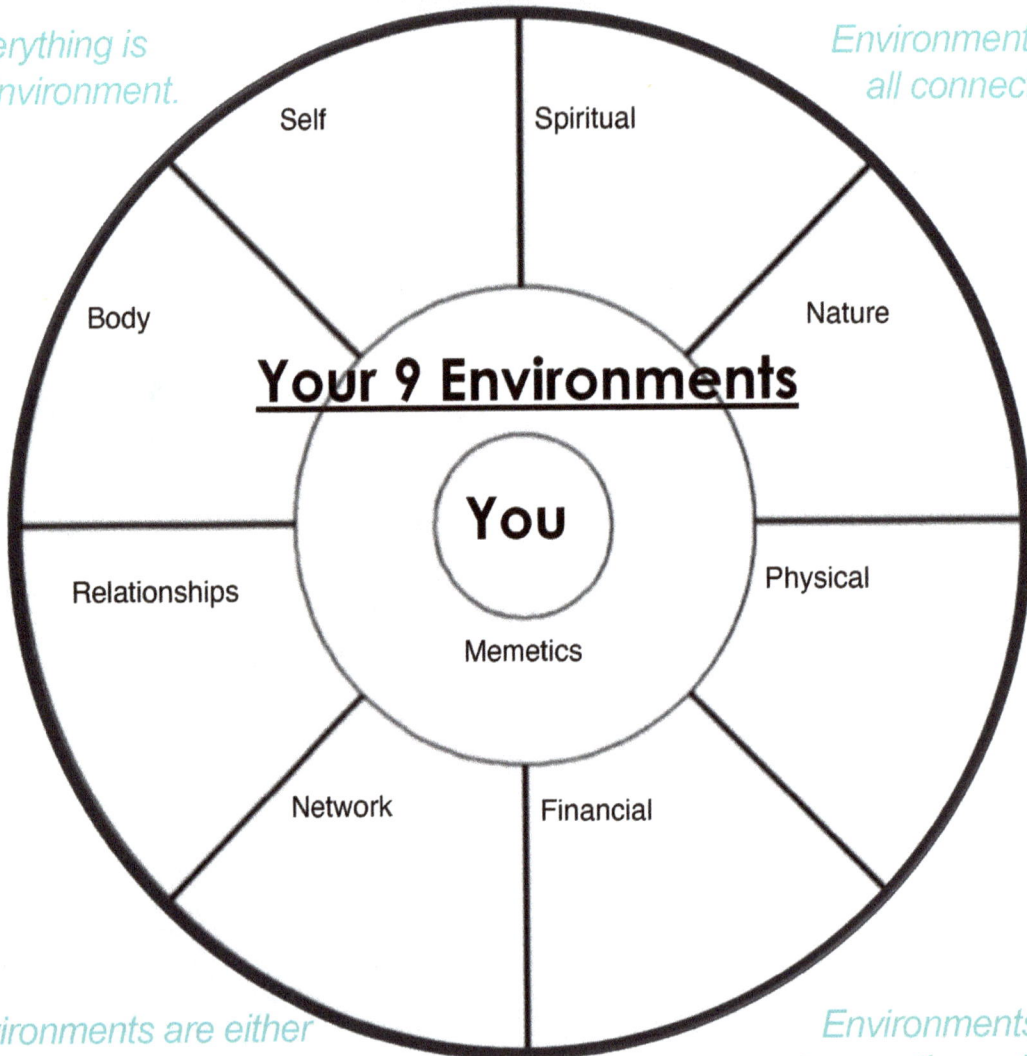

Your 9 Environments

Self

Spiritual

Body

Nature

You

Relationships

Memetics

Physical

Network

Financial

Environments are either inspiring you or expiring you.

Environments are stronger than willpower.

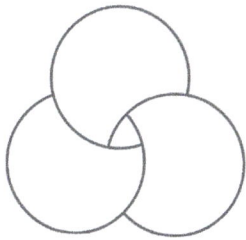

ultimate life

Inspiration / Expiration
Exercise

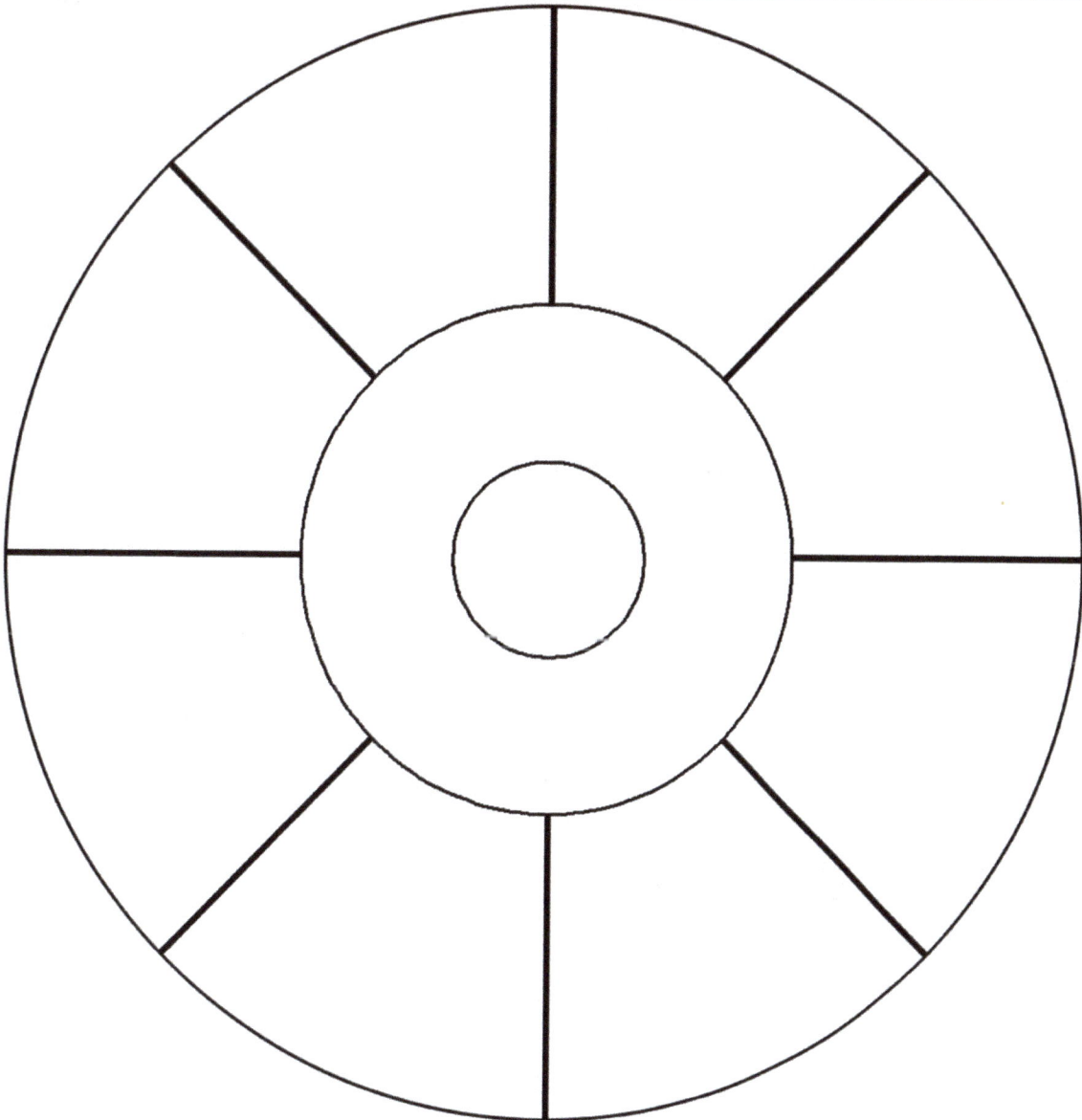

Scorecard / Habit Tracker

Happy Goal _____

Healthy Goal _____

Wealthy Goal _____

ultimate life

Week starting _____ Accountability Partner Name/# _____

DAILY ACTIONS

Happy Habits / Actions	Mon	Tues	Wed	Thurs	Fri

Healthy Habits / Actions	Mon	Tues	Wed	Thurs	Fri

Wealthy Habits / Actions	Mon	Tues	Wed	Thurs	Fri

⚙ Committed Habit   ☺ Completed Habit   ☒ Incomplete Habit   ☑ Bonus Habit

WEEKLY TOTAL 0

Power Up

AFFIRMATIONS

TODAY'S MANTRA

TODAY'S THOUGHTS

_____
_____
_____
_____
_____
_____
_____
_____
_____
_____

BRIGHT IDEAS

_____
_____
_____
_____

3 Commitments	Habits	How I Will Lead
H:	Start:	Myself:
H:	Stop:	
W:	Continue:	Others:

Everything is an environment, and environments are all connected.

TOP 3 PRIORITIES

Power Play

Date ___ / ___
SMTWTFS

1.

2.

3.

6:00	1:00
6:30	1:30
7:00	2:00
7:30	2:30
8:00	3:00
8:30	3:30
9:00	4:00
9:30	4:30
10:00	5:00
10:30	5:30
11:00	6:00
11:30	6:30
12:00	7:00
12:30	7:30

Impact

Opportunity

Connection

Stay hydrated!

Step goal: _____ Steps completed: _____ Movement goal: _____

NOTES

_____

_____

_____

_____

_____

_____

_____

_____

_____

_____

_____

_____

_____

_____

_____

_____

_____

_____

_____

_____

_____

To Do	Shopping List	Appointments to Make

Power Down

GRATITUDE

NAILED IT!

REFLECTION

_____
_____
_____
_____
_____
_____
_____
_____
_____
_____

AWARENESS

_____
_____
_____
_____

Commitments Completed	Today's Wins	My HHW Score & Why
H:		H: 1 2 3 4 5
		_____
		_____
H:		H: 1 2 3 4 5
		_____
		_____
W:		W: 1 2 3 4 5
		_____
		_____
		Daily Total: _____

AFFIRMATIONS

TODAY'S MANTRA

TODAY'S THOUGHTS

_____
_____
_____
_____
_____
_____
_____
_____
_____

BRIGHT IDEAS

_____
_____
_____
_____

3 Commitments	Habits	How I Will Lead
H:	Start:	Myself:
H:	Stop:	
		Others:
W:	Continue:	

Environments can either inspire or expire you.

TOP 3 PRIORITIES

Power Play

Date ___ / ___
SMTWTFS

CALLS:
To make   To return

1.

2.

3.

6:00		1:00
6:30		1:30
7:00		2:00
7:30		2:30
8:00		3:00
8:30		3:30
9:00		4:00
9:30		4:30
10:00		5:00
10:30		5:30
11:00		6:00
11:30		6:30
12:00		7:00
12:30		7:30

Impact

Opportunity

Connection

Stay hydrated!

Step goal: _____   Steps completed: _____   Movement goal: _____

NOTES

_____
_____
_____
_____
_____
_____
_____
_____
_____
_____
_____
_____
_____
_____
_____
_____
_____
_____
_____
_____
_____

To Do	Shopping List	Appointments to Make

Power Down

GRATITUDE

NAILED IT!

REFLECTION

_____
_____
_____
_____
_____
_____
_____
_____
_____
_____

AWARENESS

_____
_____
_____
_____

Commitments Completed

H:

H:

W:

Today's Wins

My HHW Score & Why

H: 1 2 3 4 5
_____
_____

H: 1 2 3 4 5
_____
_____

W: 1 2 3 4 5
_____
_____

Daily Total: _____

Power Up

Date ____ / ____

SMTWTFS

TODAY'S MANTRA

TODAY'S THOUGHTS

_____

_____

_____

_____

_____

_____

_____

_____

_____

BRIGHT IDEAS

_____

_____

_____

_____

3 Commitments	Habits	How I Will Lead
H:	Start:	Myself:
H:	Stop:	Others:
W:	Continue:	

Environments are stronger than willpower.

TOP 3 PRIORITIES

1.

2.

3.

Power Play

Date ___ / ___
SMTWTFS

CALLS:

To make   To return

Time		Time	
6:00		1:00	
6:30		1:30	
7:00		2:00	
7:30		2:30	
8:00		3:00	
8:30		3:30	
9:00		4:00	
9:30		4:30	
10:00		5:00	
10:30		5:30	
11:00		6:00	
11:30		6:30	
12:00		7:00	
12:30		7:30	

Impact

Opportunity

Connection

Stay hydrated!

Step goal: _____   Steps completed: _____   Movement goal: _____

NOTES

_____

_____

_____

_____

_____

_____

_____

_____

_____

_____

_____

_____

_____

_____

_____

_____

_____

_____

_____

_____

_____

To Do	Shopping List	Appointments to Make

Power Down

GRATITUDE

NAILED IT!

REFLECTION

_____
_____
_____
_____
_____
_____
_____
_____
_____
_____

AWARENESS

_____
_____
_____
_____

Commitments Completed

H:

H:

W:

Today's Wins

My HHW Score & Why

H: 1 2 3 4 5
_____
_____

H: 1 2 3 4 5
_____
_____

W: 1 2 3 4 5
_____
_____

Daily Total: _____

AFFIRMATIONS

Power Up

Date ___ / ___
SMTWTFS

TODAY'S MANTRA

TODAY'S THOUGHTS

_____
_____
_____
_____
_____
_____
_____
_____
_____
_____

BRIGHT IDEAS

_____
_____
_____
_____

3 Commitments	Habits	How I Will Lead
H:	Start:	Myself:
H:	Stop:	
		Others:
W:	Continue:	

"You can't make positive choices for the rest of your life without an environment that makes those choices easy, natural, and enjoyable."
~ Deepak Chopra

TOP 3 PRIORITIES

Power Play

Date ___ / ___
SMTWTFS

CALLS:

To make   To return

1.

2.

3.

6:00 _____		1:00 _____
6:30 _____		1:30 _____
7:00 _____		2:00 _____
7:30 _____		2:30 _____
8:00 _____		3:00 _____
8:30 _____		3:30 _____
9:00 _____		4:00 _____
9:30 _____		4:30 _____
10:00 _____		5:00 _____
10:30 _____		5:30 _____
11:00 _____		6:00 _____
11:30 _____		6:30 _____
12:00 _____		7:00 _____
12:30 _____		7:30 _____

Impact   Opportunity   Connection

Stay hydrated!

Step goal: _____   Steps completed: _____   Movement goal: _____

NOTES

_____
_____
_____
_____
_____
_____
_____
_____
_____
_____
_____
_____
_____
_____
_____
_____
_____
_____
_____
_____
_____
_____

To Do   Shopping List   Appointments to Make

Power Down

GRATITUDE

NAILED IT!

REFLECTION

_____
_____
_____
_____
_____
_____
_____
_____
_____
_____

AWARENESS

_____
_____
_____
_____

Commitments Completed

H:

H:

W:

Today's Wins

My HHW Score & Why

H: 1 2 3 4 5
_____
_____

H: 1 2 3 4 5
_____
_____

W: 1 2 3 4 5
_____
_____

Daily Total: _____

Power Up

AFFIRMATIONS

TODAY'S MANTRA

Date ___ / ___
SMTWTFS

TODAY'S THOUGHTS

_____
_____
_____
_____
_____
_____
_____
_____
_____
_____

BRIGHT IDEAS

_____
_____
_____
_____

3 Commitments	Habits	How I Will Lead
H:	Start:	Myself:
H:	Stop:	Others:
W:	Continue:	

_"When a flower doesn't bloom you fix the environment
in which it grows, not the flower."
~ Alexander Den Heijer_

TOP 3 PRIORITIES

Power Play

1.

2.

3.

Date ___ / ___
SMTWTFS

6:00 _____	1:00 _____
6:30 _____	1:30 _____
7:00 _____	2:00 _____
7:30 _____	2:30 _____
8:00 _____	3:00 _____
8:30 _____	3:30 _____
9:00 _____	4:00 _____
9:30 _____	4:30 _____
10:00 _____	5:00 _____
10:30 _____	5:30 _____
11:00 _____	6:00 _____
11:30 _____	6:30 _____
12:00 _____	7:00 _____
12:30 _____	7:30 _____

Impact   Opportunity   Connection

Stay hydrated!

Step goal: _____   Steps completed: _____   Movement goal: _____

NOTES

_____

_____

_____

_____

_____

_____

_____

_____

_____

_____

_____

_____

_____

_____

_____

_____

_____

_____

_____

_____

To Do	Shopping List	Appointments to Make

Power Down

GRATITUDE

NAILED IT!

REFLECTION

_____
_____
_____
_____
_____
_____
_____
_____
_____
_____

AWARENESS

_____
_____
_____
_____

Commitments Completed	Today's Wins	My HHW Score & Why
H:		H: 1 2 3 4 5
		_____
		_____
H:		H: 1 2 3 4 5
		_____
		_____
W:		W: 1 2 3 4 5
		_____
		_____
		Daily Total: _____

AFFIRMATIONS

Power Up

Date ___ / ___
SMTWTFS

TODAY'S MANTRA

TODAY'S THOUGHTS

_____
_____
_____
_____
_____
_____
_____
_____
_____
_____

BRIGHT IDEAS

_____
_____
_____
_____

3 Commitments	Habits	How I Will Lead
H:	Start:	Myself:
H:	Stop:	
		Others:
W:	Continue:	

"If you set up the right environment, you will literally be pulled toward your goals."
~ Thomas Leonard

TOP 3 PRIORITIES

Power Play

CALLS:
To make   To return

Date ___ / ___
SMTWTFS

1.

2.

3.

6:00	1:00
6:30	1:30
7:00	2:00
7:30	2:30
8:00	3:00
8:30	3:30
9:00	4:00
9:30	4:30
10:00	5:00
10:30	5:30
11:00	6:00
11:30	6:30
12:00	7:00
12:30	7:30

Impact   Opportunity   Connection

Stay hydrated!

Step goal: _____   Steps completed: _____   Movement goal: _____

NOTES

_____
_____
_____
_____
_____
_____
_____
_____
_____
_____
_____
_____
_____
_____
_____
_____
_____
_____
_____
_____

To Do	Shopping List	Appointments to Make

Power Down

GRATITUDE

NAILED IT!

REFLECTION

_____
_____
_____
_____
_____
_____
_____
_____
_____
_____

AWARENESS

_____
_____
_____
_____

Commitments Completed

H:

H:

W:

Today's Wins

My HHW Score & Why

H: 1 2 3 4 5
_____
_____

H: 1 2 3 4 5
_____
_____

W: 1 2 3 4 5
_____
_____

Daily Total: _____

Power Up

AFFIRMATIONS

TODAY'S MANTRA

Date ___ / ___
SMTWTFS

TODAY'S THOUGHTS

_____
_____
_____
_____
_____
_____
_____
_____
_____

BRIGHT IDEAS

_____
_____
_____
_____

3 Commitments	Habits	How I Will Lead
H:	Start:	Myself:
H:	Stop:	
		Others:
W:	Continue:	

"Live life by design, not by default."
~ Ultimate Life

TOP 3 PRIORITIES

1.

2.

3.

Power Play

Date ___ / ___
SMTWTFS

CALLS:
To make   To return

6:00	_____	1:00	_____
6:30	_____	1:30	_____
7:00	_____	2:00	_____
7:30	_____	2:30	_____
8:00	_____	3:00	_____
8:30	_____	3:30	_____
9:00	_____	4:00	_____
9:30	_____	4:30	_____
10:00	_____	5:00	_____
10:30	_____	5:30	_____
11:00	_____	6:00	_____
11:30	_____	6:30	_____
12:00	_____	7:00	_____
12:30	_____	7:30	_____

Impact

Opportunity

Connection

Stay hydrated!

Step goal: _____   Steps completed: _____   Movement goal: _____

NOTES

_____

_____

_____

_____

_____

_____

_____

_____

_____

_____

_____

_____

_____

_____

_____

_____

_____

_____

_____

_____

To Do	Shopping List	Appointments to Make

Power Down

GRATITUDE

NAILED IT!

REFLECTION

_____
_____
_____
_____
_____
_____
_____
_____
_____
_____

AWARENESS

_____
_____
_____
_____

Commitments Completed	Today's Wins	My HHW Score & Why
H:		H: 1 2 3 4 5
		_____
		_____
H:		H: 1 2 3 4 5
		_____
		_____
W:		W: 1 2 3 4 5
		_____
		_____
		Daily Total: _____

06 BUILDING YOUR SUCCESS FOUNDATION

"Most people overestimate what they can do in a short amount of time and underestimate what they can accomplish in a long period of time."

week six

week six
BUILDING YOUR
SUCCESS FOUNDATION

FOUNDATIONS 06 FOR SUCCESS

What are some actions you can take to build a Solid and Sustainable Foundation?

There are several action steps you can implement into your life to help you build a strong foundation for your future. Here are some action steps you can take to build your foundation:

- Plan ahead and block time
- Be diligent about putting the proper pillars in place in your life
- Build a strong support system
- Establish strong boundaries with yourself and others. Learn to say no.
- Create powerful daily habits.
- Creating recreation in our lives - "re-creating" by stopping and looking at what you are doing now and then creating something new.

We are all setting an example by how we live our lives, by either what "to do" or what "not to do."

_____

_____

_____

_____

_____

_____

Scorecard / Habit Tracker

Happy Goal _____

Healthy Goal _____

Wealthy Goal _____

ultimate life

Week starting _____ Accountability Partner Name/# _____

DAILY ACTIONS

Happy Habits / Actions	Mon	Tues	Wed	Thurs	Fri

Healthy Habits / Actions	Mon	Tues	Wed	Thurs	Fri

Wealthy Habits / Actions	Mon	Tues	Wed	Thurs	Fri

⚙ Committed Habit ☺ Completed Habit ☒ Incomplete Habit ☑ Bonus Habit

WEEKLY TOTAL | **0**

AFFIRMATIONS

Power Up

Date ___ / ___
SMTWTFS

TODAY'S MANTRA

TODAY'S THOUGHTS

_____
_____
_____
_____
_____
_____
_____
_____
_____
_____

BRIGHT IDEAS

_____
_____
_____
_____

3 Commitments	Habits	How I Will Lead
H:	Start:	Myself:
H:	Stop:	Others:
W:	Continue:	

If you want to build something that is stable and which lasts,
you have to invest in the foundation.

TOP 3 PRIORITIES

Power Play

CALLS:

To make   To return

1.

2.

3.

Date ___ / ___
SMTWTFS

6:00	1:00
6:30	1:30
7:00	2:00
7:30	2:30
8:00	3:00
8:30	3:30
9:00	4:00
9:30	4:30
10:00	5:00
10:30	5:30
11:00	6:00
11:30	6:30
12:00	7:00
12:30	7:30

Impact

Opportunity

Connection

Stay hydrated!

Step goal: _____   Steps completed: _____   Movement goal: _____

NOTES

_____

_____

_____

_____

_____

_____

_____

_____

_____

_____

_____

_____

_____

_____

_____

_____

_____

_____

_____

_____

_____

To Do	Shopping List	Appointments to Make

Power Down

GRATITUDE

NAILED IT!

REFLECTION

_____
_____
_____
_____
_____
_____
_____
_____
_____
_____

AWARENESS

_____
_____
_____
_____

Commitments Completed

H:

H:

W:

Today's Wins

My HHW Score & Why

H: 1 2 3 4 5
_____
_____

H: 1 2 3 4 5
_____
_____

W: 1 2 3 4 5
_____
_____

Daily Total: _____

Power Up

AFFIRMATIONS

Date ___ / ___
SMTWTFS

TODAY'S MANTRA

TODAY'S THOUGHTS

_____
_____
_____
_____
_____
_____
_____
_____
_____
_____

BRIGHT IDEAS

_____
_____
_____
_____

3 Commitments	Habits	How I Will Lead
H:	Start:	Myself:
H:	Stop:	
		Others:
W:	Continue:	

"Just like a great building stands on a strong foundation, so does success.
And the foundation of success is attitude."
~ Shiv Khera

TOP 3 PRIORITIES

Power Play

CALLS:

To make   To return

1.

2.

3.

Date ___ / ___
SMTWTFS

6:00 _____	1:00 _____
6:30 _____	1:30 _____
7:00 _____	2:00 _____
7:30 _____	2:30 _____
8:00 _____	3:00 _____
8:30 _____	3:30 _____
9:00 _____	4:00 _____
9:30 _____	4:30 _____
10:00 _____	5:00 _____
10:30 _____	5:30 _____
11:00 _____	6:00 _____
11:30 _____	6:30 _____
12:00 _____	7:00 _____
12:30 _____	7:30 _____

Impact   Opportunity   Connection

Stay hydrated!

Step goal: _____   Steps completed: _____   Movement goal: _____

NOTES

_____
_____
_____
_____
_____
_____
_____
_____
_____
_____
_____
_____
_____
_____
_____
_____
_____
_____
_____

To Do	Shopping List	Appointments to Make

Power Down

GRATITUDE

NAILED IT!

REFLECTION

_____
_____
_____
_____
_____
_____
_____
_____
_____
_____

AWARENESS

_____
_____
_____
_____

Commitments Completed

H:

H:

W:

Today's Wins

My HHW Score & Why

H: 1 2 3 4 5
_____
_____

H: 1 2 3 4 5
_____
_____

W: 1 2 3 4 5
_____
_____

Daily Total: _____

Power Up

AFFIRMATIONS

TODAY'S MANTRA

Date ___ / ___
SMTWTFS

TODAY'S THOUGHTS

_____
_____
_____
_____
_____
_____
_____
_____
_____
_____

BRIGHT IDEAS

_____
_____
_____
_____

3 Commitments	Habits	How I Will Lead
H:	Start:	Myself:
H:	Stop:	
W:	Continue:	Others:

"It is not the beauty of a building you should look at; it's the construction of the foundation that will stand the test of time."
~ David Allen Coe

TOP 3 PRIORITIES

1.

2.

3.

Power Play

Date ___ / ___
SMTWTFS

CALLS:
To make   To return

6:00	_____	1:00	_____
6:30	_____	1:30	_____
7:00	_____	2:00	_____
7:30	_____	2:30	_____
8:00	_____	3:00	_____
8:30	_____	3:30	_____
9:00	_____	4:00	_____
9:30	_____	4:30	_____
10:00	_____	5:00	_____
10:30	_____	5:30	_____
11:00	_____	6:00	_____
11:30	_____	6:30	_____
12:00	_____	7:00	_____
12:30	_____	7:30	_____

Impact   Opportunity   Connection

Stay hydrated!

Step goal: _____   Steps completed: _____   Movement goal: _____

NOTES

_____
_____
_____
_____
_____
_____
_____
_____
_____
_____
_____
_____
_____
_____
_____
_____
_____
_____
_____
_____

To Do	Shopping List	Appointments to Make

Power Down

GRATITUDE

NAILED IT!

REFLECTION

_____
_____
_____
_____
_____
_____
_____
_____
_____
_____

AWARENESS

_____
_____
_____
_____

Commitments Completed

H:

H:

W:

Today's Wins

My HHW Score & Why

H: 1 2 3 4 5
_____
_____

H: 1 2 3 4 5
_____
_____

W: 1 2 3 4 5
_____
_____

Daily Total: _____

Power Up

AFFIRMATIONS

TODAY'S MANTRA

Date ___ / ___
SMTWTFS

TODAY'S THOUGHTS

_____
_____
_____
_____
_____
_____
_____
_____
_____
_____

BRIGHT IDEAS

_____
_____
_____
_____

3 Commitments	Habits	How I Will Lead
H:	Start:	Myself:
H:	Stop:	
W:	Continue:	Others:

"Most people overestimate what they can do in a short amount of time and underestimate what they can accomplish in a long period of time."

TOP 3 PRIORITIES

1.

2.

3.

Power Play

Date ___ / ___
SMTWTFS

CALLS:
To make   To return

6:00	1:00
6:30	1:30
7:00	2:00
7:30	2:30
8:00	3:00
8:30	3:30
9:00	4:00
9:30	4:30
10:00	5:00
10:30	5:30
11:00	6:00
11:30	6:30
12:00	7:00
12:30	7:30

Impact   Opportunity   Connection

Stay hydrated!

Step goal: _____   Steps completed: _____   Movement goal: _____

NOTES

_____
_____
_____
_____
_____
_____
_____
_____
_____
_____
_____
_____
_____
_____
_____
_____
_____
_____
_____
_____

To Do   Shopping List   Appointments to Make

Power Down

GRATITUDE

NAILED IT!

REFLECTION

_____
_____
_____
_____
_____
_____
_____
_____
_____
_____

AWARENESS

_____
_____
_____
_____

Commitments Completed	Today's Wins	My HHW Score & Why
H: H: W:		H: 1 2 3 4 5 _____ _____ H: 1 2 3 4 5 _____ _____ W: 1 2 3 4 5 _____ _____ Daily Total: _____

Power Up

AFFIRMATIONS

TODAY'S MANTRA

TODAY'S THOUGHTS

_____
_____
_____
_____
_____
_____
_____
_____
_____
_____

BRIGHT IDEAS

_____
_____
_____
_____

3 Commitments	Habits	How I Will Lead
H:	Start:	Myself:
H:	Stop:	
		Others:
W:	Continue:	

"If you build it, they will come."
~ Field of Dreams

TOP 3 PRIORITIES

Power Play

Date ___ / ___
SMTWTFS

CALLS:
To make   To return

1.

2.

3.

6:00	1:00
6:30	1:30
7:00	2:00
7:30	2:30
8:00	3:00
8:30	3:30
9:00	4:00
9:30	4:30
10:00	5:00
10:30	5:30
11:00	6:00
11:30	6:30
12:00	7:00
12:30	7:30

Impact   Opportunity   Connection

Stay hydrated!

Step goal: _____   Steps completed: _____   Movement goal: _____

NOTES

_____
_____
_____
_____
_____
_____
_____
_____
_____
_____
_____
_____
_____
_____
_____
_____
_____
_____
_____
_____
_____
_____

To Do   Shopping List   Appointments to Make

Power Down

GRATITUDE

NAILED IT!

REFLECTION

_____
_____
_____
_____
_____
_____
_____
_____
_____
_____

AWARENESS

_____
_____
_____
_____

Commitments Completed

H:

H:

W:

Today's Wins

My HHW Score & Why

H: 1 2 3 4 5

_____
_____

H: 1 2 3 4 5

_____
_____

W: 1 2 3 4 5

_____
_____

Daily Total: _____

Power Up

AFFIRMATIONS

Date ___ / ___

SMTWTFS

TODAY'S MANTRA

TODAY'S THOUGHTS

_____
_____
_____
_____
_____
_____
_____
_____
_____
_____

BRIGHT IDEAS

_____
_____
_____
_____

3 Commitments	Habits	How I Will Lead
H:	Start:	Myself:
H:	Stop:	Others:
W:	Continue:	

*"If you want to find the secrets of the universe,
think in terms of energy, frequency and vibration."
~ Nikola Tesla*

TOP 3 PRIORITIES

1.

2.

3.

Power Play

Date ___ / ___

SMTWTFS

CALLS:

To make   To return

Time		Time	
6:00	_____	1:00	_____
6:30	_____	1:30	_____
7:00	_____	2:00	_____
7:30	_____	2:30	_____
8:00	_____	3:00	_____
8:30	_____	3:30	_____
9:00	_____	4:00	_____
9:30	_____	4:30	_____
10:00	_____	5:00	_____
10:30	_____	5:30	_____
11:00	_____	6:00	_____
11:30	_____	6:30	_____
12:00	_____	7:00	_____
12:30	_____	7:30	_____

Impact

Opportunity

Connection

Stay hydrated!

Step goal: _____   Steps completed: _____   Movement goal: _____

NOTES

_____
_____
_____
_____
_____
_____
_____
_____
_____
_____
_____
_____
_____
_____
_____
_____
_____
_____
_____
_____

To Do	Shopping List	Appointments to Make

Power Down

GRATITUDE

NAILED IT!

REFLECTION

_____
_____
_____
_____
_____
_____
_____
_____
_____
_____

AWARENESS

_____
_____
_____
_____

Commitments Completed

H:

H:

W:

Today's Wins

My HHW Score & Why

H: 1 2 3 4 5
_____
_____

H: 1 2 3 4 5
_____
_____

W: 1 2 3 4 5
_____
_____

Daily Total: _____

AFFIRMATIONS

Power Up

Date ___ / ___
SMTWTFS

TODAY'S MANTRA

TODAY'S THOUGHTS

_____
_____
_____
_____
_____
_____
_____
_____
_____
_____

BRIGHT IDEAS

_____
_____
_____
_____

3 Commitments	Habits	How I Will Lead
H:	Start:	Myself:
H:	Stop:	
		Others:
W:	Continue:	

"Now it comes down to one simple choice... Do you want it?"
~ Gina Pigott

TOP 3 PRIORITIES

1.

2.

3.

Power Play

Date ___ / ___

SMTWTFS

CALLS:

To make   To return

Time		Time	
6:00		1:00	
6:30		1:30	
7:00		2:00	
7:30		2:30	
8:00		3:00	
8:30		3:30	
9:00		4:00	
9:30		4:30	
10:00		5:00	
10:30		5:30	
11:00		6:00	
11:30		6:30	
12:00		7:00	
12:30		7:30	

Impact

Opportunity

Connection

Stay hydrated!

Step goal: _____   Steps completed: _____   Movement goal: _____

NOTES

_____
_____
_____
_____
_____
_____
_____
_____
_____
_____
_____
_____
_____
_____
_____
_____
_____
_____
_____
_____

To Do	Shopping List	Appointments to Make

Power Down

GRATITUDE

NAILED IT!

REFLECTION

_____
_____
_____
_____
_____
_____
_____
_____
_____

AWARENESS

_____
_____
_____
_____

Commitments Completed	Today's Wins	My HHW Score & Why
H:		H: 1 2 3 4 5
		_____
		_____
H:		H: 1 2 3 4 5
		_____
		_____
W:		W: 1 2 3 4 5
		_____
		_____
		Daily Total: _____

07 LIVING A VALUES DRIVEN LIFE

"All of us are trying to get down to, what are your core
values? ...If you'll play for any team that
asks you to play, it raises the questions of where would
you draw the line, if you would draw the line."
~ Richard Durbin

week seven

week seven

LIVING A VALUES DRIVEN LIFE

_____

_____

_____

_____

_____

_____

_____

_____

_____

_____

_____

_____

_____

_____

_____

_____

_____

_____

There are many values assessments.
Begin with a complimentary personal values
assessment here by clicking on the QR code.

KNOW YOUR VALUES
07

Core values are the deeply ingrained principles/beliefs which drive your actions. They are the glue that is holding your life together, and they are principles you will discover by looking deeply inside your life...not by looking outside of you.

Developing core values is easy. Living according to them is not quite so easy. It takes GUTS! Once you develop your core values, you must be willing to be intolerant of the people in your life violating them. You must be willing to feel some type of reaction (both positive and negative) from the public when you put your stake in the ground around your values; otherwise, there is no point in having core values for your life.

Core values can distinguish you as a unique leader in the world. They can set you apart from others and can serve as a rallying point for others.

Core values are discovered by looking inside at what makes you tick...at what truly inspires you in the deepest part of your soul. You cannot fake core values, and you cannot buy them from a book or find them outside of you. While the environment can inspire you to connect with your values, it is very difficult to find them "out there." You must be willing to look inside and be ruthlessly honest with yourself in defining what really matters most to you in life. Values do not have to be "appropriate." They do, however, have to be authentic for you.

Scorecard / Habit Tracker

Happy Goal _____

Healthy Goal _____

Wealthy Goal _____

Week starting _____ Accountability Partner Name/# _____

ultimate life

DAILY ACTIONS

Happy Habits / Actions	Mon	Tues	Wed	Thurs	Fri

Healthy Habits / Actions	Mon	Tues	Wed	Thurs	Fri

Wealthy Habits / Actions	Mon	Tues	Wed	Thurs	Fri

Committed Habit   Completed Habit   Incomplete Habit   Bonus Habit

WEEKLY TOTAL | 0

Power Up

AFFIRMATIONS

TODAY'S MANTRA

Date ____ / ____

SMTWTFS

TODAY'S THOUGHTS

_____

_____

_____

_____

_____

_____

_____

_____

_____

_____

BRIGHT IDEAS

_____

_____

_____

_____

3 Commitments	Habits	How I Will Lead
H:	Start:	Myself:
H:	Stop:	
		Others:
W:	Continue:	

"It's not hard to make decisions once you know what your values are."
~ Roy Disney

TOP 3 PRIORITIES

Power Play

CALLS:
To make   To return

1.

2.

3.

Date ___ / ___
SMTWTFS

6:00 _____	1:00 _____
6:30 _____	1:30 _____
7:00 _____	2:00 _____
7:30 _____	2:30 _____
8:00 _____	3:00 _____
8:30 _____	3:30 _____
9:00 _____	4:00 _____
9:30 _____	4:30 _____
10:00 _____	5:00 _____
10:30 _____	5:30 _____
11:00 _____	6:00 _____
11:30 _____	6:30 _____
12:00 _____	7:00 _____
12:30 _____	7:30 _____

Impact   Opportunity   Connection

Stay hydrated!

Step goal: _____   Steps completed: _____   Movement goal: _____

NOTES

_____
_____
_____
_____
_____
_____
_____
_____
_____
_____
_____
_____
_____
_____
_____
_____
_____
_____
_____
_____

To Do	Shopping List	Appointments to Make

Power Down

GRATITUDE

NAILED IT!

REFLECTION

_____
_____
_____
_____
_____
_____
_____
_____
_____
_____

AWARENESS

_____
_____
_____
_____

Commitments Completed

H:

H:

W:

Today's Wins

My HHW Score & Why

H: 1 2 3 4 5
_____
_____

H: 1 2 3 4 5
_____
_____

W: 1 2 3 4 5
_____
_____

Daily Total: _____

AFFIRMATIONS

Power Up

Date ___ / ___
SMTWTFS

TODAY'S MANTRA

TODAY'S THOUGHTS

_____
_____
_____
_____
_____
_____
_____
_____
_____
_____

BRIGHT IDEAS

_____
_____
_____
_____

3 Commitments

H:

H:

W:

Habits

Start:

Stop:

Continue:

How I Will Lead

Myself:

Others:

"Knowing yourself is the beginning of all wisdom."
~ Aristotle

TOP 3 PRIORITIES

1.

2.

3.

Power Play

Date ___ / ___

SMTWTFS

CALLS:

To make   To return

6:00	1:00
6:30	1:30
7:00	2:00
7:30	2:30
8:00	3:00
8:30	3:30
9:00	4:00
9:30	4:30
10:00	5:00
10:30	5:30
11:00	6:00
11:30	6:30
12:00	7:00
12:30	7:30

Impact   Opportunity   Connection

Stay hydrated!

Step goal: _____   Steps completed: _____   Movement goal: _____

NOTES

_____

_____

_____

_____

_____

_____

_____

_____

_____

_____

_____

_____

_____

_____

_____

_____

_____

_____

_____

_____

_____

To Do	Shopping List	Appointments to Make

Power Down

GRATITUDE

NAILED IT!

REFLECTION

_____
_____
_____
_____
_____
_____
_____
_____
_____
_____

AWARENESS

_____
_____
_____
_____

Commitments Completed

H:

H:

W:

Today's Wins

My HHW Score & Why

H: 1 2 3 4 5
_____
_____

H: 1 2 3 4 5
_____
_____

W: 1 2 3 4 5
_____
_____

Daily Total: _____

AFFIRMATIONS

Power Up

Date ___ / ___
SMTWTFS

TODAY'S MANTRA

TODAY'S THOUGHTS

_____
_____
_____
_____
_____
_____
_____
_____
_____
_____

BRIGHT IDEAS

_____
_____
_____
_____

3 Commitments	Habits	How I Will Lead
H:	Start:	Myself:
H:	Stop:	Others:
W:	Continue:	

*"Your core values act like your internal compass,
which navigates the course of your life."*
~ Roy T. Bennett

TOP 3 PRIORITIES

Power Play

CALLS:

To make   To return

1.

2.

3.

Date ___ / ___
SMTWTFS

6:00	_____	1:00	_____
6:30	_____	1:30	_____
7:00	_____	2:00	_____
7:30	_____	2:30	_____
8:00	_____	3:00	_____
8:30	_____	3:30	_____
9:00	_____	4:00	_____
9:30	_____	4:30	_____
10:00	_____	5:00	_____
10:30	_____	5:30	_____
11:00	_____	6:00	_____
11:30	_____	6:30	_____
12:00	_____	7:00	_____
12:30	_____	7:30	_____

Impact

Opportunity

Connection

Stay hydrated!

Step goal: _____   Steps completed: _____   Movement goal: _____

NOTES

_____

_____

_____

_____

_____

_____

_____

_____

_____

_____

_____

_____

_____

_____

_____

_____

_____

_____

_____

_____

_____

To Do	Shopping List	Appointments to Make

Power Down

GRATITUDE

NAILED IT!

REFLECTION

_____
_____
_____
_____
_____
_____
_____
_____
_____
_____

AWARENESS

_____
_____
_____
_____

Commitments Completed

H:

H:

W:

Today's Wins

My HHW Score & Why

H: 1 2 3 4 5
_____
_____

H: 1 2 3 4 5
_____
_____

W: 1 2 3 4 5
_____
_____

Daily Total: _____

Power Up

Date ____ / ____
SMTWTFS

AFFIRMATIONS

TODAY'S MANTRA

TODAY'S THOUGHTS

_____
_____
_____
_____
_____
_____
_____
_____
_____
_____

BRIGHT IDEAS

_____
_____
_____
_____

3 Commitments	Habits	How I Will Lead
H:	Start:	Myself:
H:	Stop:	
W:	Continue:	Others:

"It takes courage to grow up and become who you really are."
~ e.e. cummings

TOP 3 PRIORITIES

Power Play

CALLS:

To make   To return

1.

Date ___ / ___
SMTWTFS

2.

3.

6:00	1:00
6:30	1:30
7:00	2:00
7:30	2:30
8:00	3:00
8:30	3:30
9:00	4:00
9:30	4:30
10:00	5:00
10:30	5:30
11:00	6:00
11:30	6:30
12:00	7:00
12:30	7:30

Impact   Opportunity   Connection

Stay hydrated!

Step goal: _____   Steps completed: _____   Movement goal: _____

NOTES

_____
_____
_____
_____
_____
_____
_____
_____
_____
_____
_____
_____
_____
_____
_____
_____
_____
_____
_____
_____
_____

To Do	Shopping List	Appointments to Make

Power Down

GRATITUDE

NAILED IT!

REFLECTION

_____
_____
_____
_____
_____
_____
_____
_____
_____
_____

AWARENESS

_____
_____
_____
_____

Commitments Completed

H:

H:

W:

Today's Wins

My HHW Score & Why

H: 1 2 3 4 5

_____
_____

H: 1 2 3 4 5

_____
_____

W: 1 2 3 4 5

_____
_____

Daily Total: _____

Power Up

AFFIRMATIONS

Date ___ / ___
SMTWTFS

TODAY'S MANTRA

TODAY'S THOUGHTS

_____
_____
_____
_____
_____
_____
_____
_____
_____
_____

BRIGHT IDEAS

_____
_____
_____
_____

3 Commitments	Habits	How I Will Lead
H:	Start:	Myself:
H:	Stop:	
		Others:
W:	Continue:	

_"Values are like fingerprints. Nobody's are the same,
but you leave them all over everything you do."
~ Elvis Presley_

TOP 3 PRIORITIES

1.

2.

3.

Power Play

Date ___ / ___
SMTWTFS

CALLS:

To make   To return

6:00	_____	1:00	_____
6:30	_____	1:30	_____
7:00	_____	2:00	_____
7:30	_____	2:30	_____
8:00	_____	3:00	_____
8:30	_____	3:30	_____
9:00	_____	4:00	_____
9:30	_____	4:30	_____
10:00	_____	5:00	_____
10:30	_____	5:30	_____
11:00	_____	6:00	_____
11:30	_____	6:30	_____
12:00	_____	7:00	_____
12:30	_____	7:30	_____

Impact   Opportunity   Connection

Stay hydrated!

Step goal: _____   Steps completed: _____   Movement goal: _____

NOTES

To Do

Shopping List

Appointments to Make

Power Down

GRATITUDE

NAILED IT!

REFLECTION

_____
_____
_____
_____
_____
_____
_____
_____
_____
_____

AWARENESS

_____
_____
_____
_____

Commitments Completed

H:

H:

W:

Today's Wins

My HHW Score & Why

H: 1 2 3 4 5
_____
_____

H: 1 2 3 4 5
_____
_____

W: 1 2 3 4 5
_____
_____

Daily Total: _____

AFFIRMATIONS

Power Up

Date ___ / ___
SMTWTFS

TODAY'S MANTRA

TODAY'S THOUGHTS

_____
_____
_____
_____
_____
_____
_____
_____
_____
_____

BRIGHT IDEAS

_____
_____
_____
_____

3 Commitments	Habits	How I Will Lead
H:	Start:	Myself:
H:	Stop:	
		Others:
W:	Continue:	

"Change your practices without abandoning your core values."
~ James C. Collins

TOP 3 PRIORITIES

Power Play

Date ___ / ___
SMTWTFS

CALLS:
To make   To return

1.

2.

3.

6:00	_____	1:00	_____
6:30	_____	1:30	_____
7:00	_____	2:00	_____
7:30	_____	2:30	_____
8:00	_____	3:00	_____
8:30	_____	3:30	_____
9:00	_____	4:00	_____
9:30	_____	4:30	_____
10:00	_____	5:00	_____
10:30	_____	5:30	_____
11:00	_____	6:00	_____
11:30	_____	6:30	_____
12:00	_____	7:00	_____
12:30	_____	7:30	_____

Impact   Opportunity   Connection

Stay hydrated!

Step goal: _____   Steps completed: _____   Movement goal: _____

NOTES

_____
_____
_____
_____
_____
_____
_____
_____
_____
_____
_____
_____
_____
_____
_____
_____
_____
_____
_____
_____
_____
_____

To Do	Shopping List	Appointments to Make

Power Down

GRATITUDE

NAILED IT!

REFLECTION

_____
_____
_____
_____
_____
_____
_____
_____
_____

AWARENESS

_____
_____
_____
_____

Commitments Completed

H:

H:

W:

Today's Wins

My HHW Score & Why

H: 1 2 3 4 5
_____
_____

H: 1 2 3 4 5
_____
_____

W: 1 2 3 4 5
_____
_____

Daily Total: _____

AFFIRMATIONS

Power Up

Date ___ / ___
SMTWTFS

TODAY'S MANTRA

TODAY'S THOUGHTS

_____
_____
_____
_____
_____
_____
_____
_____
_____
_____

BRIGHT IDEAS

_____
_____
_____
_____

3 Commitments	Habits	How I Will Lead
H:	Start:	Myself:
H:	Stop:	
		Others:
W:	Continue:	

"When your needs are met and boundaries are placed,
you can stay focused on everything you want to accomplish."
~ Gina Pigott

TOP 3 PRIORITIES

1.

2.

3.

Power Play

Date ___ / ___
SMTWTFS

CALLS:

To make   To return

Time		Time	
6:00	_____	1:00	_____
6:30	_____	1:30	_____
7:00	_____	2:00	_____
7:30	_____	2:30	_____
8:00	_____	3:00	_____
8:30	_____	3:30	_____
9:00	_____	4:00	_____
9:30	_____	4:30	_____
10:00	_____	5:00	_____
10:30	_____	5:30	_____
11:00	_____	6:00	_____
11:30	_____	6:30	_____
12:00	_____	7:00	_____
12:30	_____	7:30	_____

Impact

Opportunity

Connection

Stay hydrated!

Step goal: _____   Steps completed: _____   Movement goal: _____

NOTES

To Do

Shopping List

Appointments to Make

Power Down

GRATITUDE

NAILED IT!

REFLECTION

_____
_____
_____
_____
_____
_____
_____
_____
_____

AWARENESS

_____
_____
_____
_____

Commitments Completed	Today's Wins	My HHW Score & Why
H:		H: 1 2 3 4 5
		_____
		_____
H:		H: 1 2 3 4 5
		_____
		_____
W:		W: 1 2 3 4 5
		_____
		_____
		Daily Total: _____

08

FOCUS AND THE LAW OF ATTRACTION

"The quality of your life is a direct reflection of the quality
of the questions you are asking yourself."
~ Anthony Robbins

week eight

week eight
FOCUS AND THE
LAW OF ATTRACTION

LAW OF ATTRACTION 08

Your Thoughts and Beliefs
create
Your Perception and Meaning
which creates
Your Feelings and Emotions
which creates
Your Motivation

That Motivation
gets You to Take Action
(or Not)
which creates

Your Results

**You can create what you want,
and you can create what you don't want!
The Universe doesn't care which,
it just delivers to you what you focus on the most.**

Scorecard / Habit Tracker

Happy Goal _____

Healthy Goal _____

Wealthy Goal _____

ultimate life

Week starting _____ **Accountability Partner Name/#** _____

					DAILY ACTIONS				
Happy Habits / Actions					Mon	Tues	Wed	Thurs	Fri
_____									
_____									
_____									
_____									
_____									
_____									
_____									
Healthy Habits / Actions					Mon	Tues	Wed	Thurs	Fri
_____									
_____									
_____									
_____									
_____									
_____									
_____									
Wealthy Habits / Actions					Mon	Tues	Wed	Thurs	Fri
_____									
_____									
_____									
_____									
_____									
_____									
_____									

⚙ Committed Habit   ☺ Completed Habit   ☒ Incomplete Habit   ☑ Bonus Habit

WEEKLY TOTAL **0**

AFFIRMATIONS

Power Up

Date ___ / ___
SMTWTFS

TODAY'S MANTRA

TODAY'S THOUGHTS

_____
_____
_____
_____
_____
_____
_____
_____
_____
_____

BRIGHT IDEAS

_____
_____
_____
_____

3 Commitments

H:

H:

W:

Habits

Start:

Stop:

Continue:

How I Will Lead

Myself:

Others:

The universe doesn't judge, it just delivers.

TOP 3 PRIORITIES

1.

2.

3.

Power Play

Date ___ / ___
SMTWTFS

6:00 _____	1:00 _____
6:30 _____	1:30 _____
7:00 _____	2:00 _____
7:30 _____	2:30 _____
8:00 _____	3:00 _____
8:30 _____	3:30 _____
9:00 _____	4:00 _____
9:30 _____	4:30 _____
10:00 _____	5:00 _____
10:30 _____	5:30 _____
11:00 _____	6:00 _____
11:30 _____	6:30 _____
12:00 _____	7:00 _____
12:30 _____	7:30 _____

Impact   Opportunity   Connection

Stay hydrated!

Step goal: _____   Steps completed: _____   Movement goal: _____

NOTES

_____
_____
_____
_____
_____
_____
_____
_____
_____
_____
_____
_____
_____
_____
_____
_____
_____
_____
_____
_____

To Do	Shopping List	Appointments to Make

Power Down

GRATITUDE

NAILED IT!

REFLECTION

_____
_____
_____
_____
_____
_____
_____
_____
_____
_____

AWARENESS

_____
_____
_____
_____

Commitments Completed

H:

H:

W:

Today's Wins

My HHW Score & Why

H: 1 2 3 4 5
_____
_____

H: 1 2 3 4 5
_____
_____

W: 1 2 3 4 5
_____
_____

Daily Total: _____

Power Up

AFFIRMATIONS

TODAY'S MANTRA

Date ____ / ____

SMTWTFS

TODAY'S THOUGHTS

_____
_____
_____
_____
_____
_____
_____
_____
_____
_____

BRIGHT IDEAS

_____
_____
_____
_____

3 Commitments	Habits	How I Will Lead
H:	Start:	Myself:
H:	Stop:	
		Others:
W:	Continue:	

"The value of knowledge is realized only when action is taken upon the knowledge.
Knowledge without action is like a seed that never grows."
~ Fran Henry

TOP 3 PRIORITIES

1.

2.

3.

Power Play

Date ___ / ___
SMTWTFS

CALLS:

To make   To return

6:00	1:00
6:30	1:30
7:00	2:00
7:30	2:30
8:00	3:00
8:30	3:30
9:00	4:00
9:30	4:30
10:00	5:00
10:30	5:30
11:00	6:00
11:30	6:30
12:00	7:00
12:30	7:30

Impact

Opportunity

Connection

Stay hydrated!

Step goal: _____   Steps completed: _____   Movement goal: _____

NOTES

_____
_____
_____
_____
_____
_____
_____
_____
_____
_____
_____
_____
_____
_____
_____
_____
_____
_____
_____
_____
_____
_____

To Do	Shopping List	Appointments to Make

Power Down

GRATITUDE

NAILED IT!

REFLECTION

_____
_____
_____
_____
_____
_____
_____
_____
_____

AWARENESS

_____
_____
_____
_____

Commitments Completed	Today's Wins	My HHW Score & Why
H:		H: 1 2 3 4 5
		_____
		_____
H:		H: 1 2 3 4 5
		_____
		_____
W:		W: 1 2 3 4 5
		_____
		_____
		Daily Total: _____

Power Up

AFFIRMATIONS

Date ___ / ___
SMTWTFS

TODAY'S MANTRA

TODAY'S THOUGHTS

_____
_____
_____
_____
_____
_____
_____
_____
_____

BRIGHT IDEAS

_____
_____
_____
_____

3 Commitments	Habits	How I Will Lead
H:	Start:	Myself:
H:	Stop:	
		Others:
W:	Continue:	

"You don't attract what you want; you attract what you are."
~ Jason Borné

TOP 3 PRIORITIES

1.

2.

3.

Power Play

Date ___ / ___

SMTWTFS

CALLS:

To make   To return

6:00 _____

6:30 _____

7:00 _____

7:30 _____

8:00 _____

8:30 _____

9:00 _____

9:30 _____

10:00 _____

10:30 _____

11:00 _____

11:30 _____

12:00 _____

12:30 _____

1:00 _____

1:30 _____

2:00 _____

2:30 _____

3:00 _____

3:30 _____

4:00 _____

4:30 _____

5:00 _____

5:30 _____

6:00 _____

6:30 _____

7:00 _____

7:30 _____

Impact

Opportunity

Connection

Stay hydrated!

Step goal: _____   Steps completed: _____   Movement goal: _____

NOTES

_____
_____
_____
_____
_____
_____
_____
_____
_____
_____
_____
_____
_____
_____
_____
_____
_____
_____
_____
_____

To Do	Shopping List	Appointments to Make

Power Down

GRATITUDE

NAILED IT!

REFLECTION

_____
_____
_____
_____
_____
_____
_____
_____
_____
_____

AWARENESS

_____
_____
_____
_____

Commitments Completed	Today's Wins	My HHW Score & Why
H:		H: 1 2 3 4 5
		_____
		_____
H:		H: 1 2 3 4 5
		_____
		_____
W:		W: 1 2 3 4 5
		_____
		_____
		Daily Total: _____

AFFIRMATIONS

Power Up

Date ___ / ___
SMTWTFS

TODAY'S MANTRA

TODAY'S THOUGHTS

_____
_____
_____
_____
_____
_____
_____
_____
_____
_____

BRIGHT IDEAS

_____
_____
_____
_____

3 Commitments

H:

H:

W:

Habits

Start:

Stop:

Continue:

How I Will Lead

Myself:

Others:

Distractions interrupt the manifestation of what you really want in your life.

TOP 3 PRIORITIES

Power Play

CALLS:

To make   To return

1.

2.

3.

Date ___ / ___
SMTWTFS

6:00		1:00
6:30		1:30
7:00		2:00
7:30		2:30
8:00		3:00
8:30		3:30
9:00		4:00
9:30		4:30
10:00		5:00
10:30		5:30
11:00		6:00
11:30		6:30
12:00		7:00
12:30		7:30

Impact

Opportunity

Connection

Stay hydrated!

Step goal: _____   Steps completed: _____   Movement goal: _____

NOTES

_____

_____

_____

_____

_____

_____

_____

_____

_____

_____

_____

_____

_____

_____

_____

_____

_____

_____

_____

_____

To Do	Shopping List	Appointments to Make

Power Down

GRATITUDE

NAILED IT!

REFLECTION

_____
_____
_____
_____
_____
_____
_____
_____
_____
_____

AWARENESS

_____
_____
_____
_____

Commitments Completed

H:

H:

W:

Today's Wins

My HHW Score & Why

H: 1 2 3 4 5
_____
_____

H: 1 2 3 4 5
_____
_____

W: 1 2 3 4 5
_____
_____

Daily Total: _____

AFFIRMATIONS

Power Up

Date ___ / ___
SMTWTFS

TODAY'S MANTRA

TODAY'S THOUGHTS

_____
_____
_____
_____
_____
_____
_____
_____
_____
_____

BRIGHT IDEAS

_____
_____
_____
_____

3 Commitments

H:

H:

W:

Habits

Start:

Stop:

Continue:

How I Will Lead

Myself:

Others:

"Whether you think you can or think you can't, either way you are right."
~ Henry Ford

TOP 3 PRIORITIES

Power Play

CALLS:
To make   To return

1.

Date ___ / ___
SMTWTFS

2.

3.

6:00		1:00
6:30		1:30
7:00		2:00
7:30		2:30
8:00		3:00
8:30		3:30
9:00		4:00
9:30		4:30
10:00		5:00
10:30		5:30
11:00		6:00
11:30		6:30
12:00		7:00
12:30		7:30

Impact   Opportunity   Connection

Stay hydrated!

Step goal: _____   Steps completed: _____   Movement goal: _____

NOTES

_____
_____
_____
_____
_____
_____
_____
_____
_____
_____
_____
_____
_____
_____
_____
_____
_____
_____
_____
_____
_____
_____

To Do   Shopping List   Appointments to Make

Power Down

GRATITUDE

NAILED IT!

REFLECTION

_____
_____
_____
_____
_____
_____
_____
_____
_____
_____

AWARENESS

_____
_____
_____
_____

Commitments Completed	Today's Wins	My HHW Score & Why
H:		H: 1 2 3 4 5
		_____
		_____
H:		H: 1 2 3 4 5
		_____
		_____
W:		W: 1 2 3 4 5
		_____
		_____
		Daily Total: _____

Power Up

AFFIRMATIONS

TODAY'S MANTRA

Date ___ / ___
SMTWTFS

TODAY'S THOUGHTS

_____
_____
_____
_____
_____
_____
_____
_____
_____
_____

BRIGHT IDEAS

_____
_____
_____
_____

3 Commitments	Habits	How I Will Lead
H:	Start:	Myself:
H:	Stop:	
		Others:
W:	Continue:	

"See yourself living in abundance and you will attract it."
~ Rhonda Byrne

TOP 3 PRIORITIES

1.

2.

3.

Power Play

Date ___ / ___
SMTWTFS

CALLS:

To make   To return

6:00	1:00
6:30	1:30
7:00	2:00
7:30	2:30
8:00	3:00
8:30	3:30
9:00	4:00
9:30	4:30
10:00	5:00
10:30	5:30
11:00	6:00
11:30	6:30
12:00	7:00
12:30	7:30

Impact   Opportunity   Connection

Stay hydrated!

Step goal: _____   Steps completed: _____   Movement goal: _____

NOTES

_____
_____
_____
_____
_____
_____
_____
_____
_____
_____
_____
_____
_____
_____
_____
_____
_____
_____
_____
_____

To Do	Shopping List	Appointments to Make

Power Down

GRATITUDE

NAILED IT!

REFLECTION

_____
_____
_____
_____
_____
_____
_____
_____
_____
_____

AWARENESS

_____
_____
_____
_____

Commitments Completed

H:

H:

W:

Today's Wins

My HHW Score & Why

H: 1 2 3 4 5
_____
_____

H: 1 2 3 4 5
_____
_____

W: 1 2 3 4 5
_____
_____

Daily Total: _____

AFFIRMATIONS

Power Up

Date ___ / ___
SMTWTFS

TODAY'S MANTRA

TODAY'S THOUGHTS

_____
_____
_____
_____
_____
_____
_____
_____
_____
_____

BRIGHT IDEAS

_____
_____
_____
_____

3 Commitments

H:

H:

W:

Habits

Start:

Stop:

Continue:

How I Will Lead

Myself:

Others:

"It's all about your next choice!"
~ Gina Pigott

TOP 3 PRIORITIES

Power Play

CALLS:
To make   To return

1.

2.

3.

Date ___ / ___
SMTWTFS

6:00	1:00
6:30	1:30
7:00	2:00
7:30	2:30
8:00	3:00
8:30	3:30
9:00	4:00
9:30	4:30
10:00	5:00
10:30	5:30
11:00	6:00
11:30	6:30
12:00	7:00
12:30	7:30

Impact

Opportunity

Connection

Stay hydrated!

Step goal: _____   Steps completed: _____   Movement goal: _____

NOTES

_____

_____

_____

_____

_____

_____

_____

_____

_____

_____

_____

_____

_____

_____

_____

_____

_____

_____

_____

_____

_____

To Do	Shopping List	Appointments to Make

Power Down

GRATITUDE

NAILED IT!

REFLECTION

_____
_____
_____
_____
_____
_____
_____
_____
_____
_____

AWARENESS

_____
_____
_____
_____

Commitments Completed	Today's Wins	My HHW Score & Why
H:		H: 1 2 3 4 5
		_____
		H: 1 2 3 4 5
H:		_____
		W: 1 2 3 4 5
W:		_____
		Daily Total: _____

09 AWARENESS IN ACTION

"How we play games,
can be a reflection of how we do life."
~ Jim Bunch

week nine

week nine

AWARENESS IN ACTION

Congratulations on Reaching Week 9!

Go back through the Planner and choose your most inspiring achievements and capture them in the spaces below.

The Momentum Exercise

Achievement	Why Important	Next Action

What happens when we don't acknowledge our wins? We burn out, lose momentum, stay stuck, and ultimately we don't perform at the level we could.

It is time to celebrate your wins and recognize yourself for all that you've done.

Scorecard / Habit Tracker

ultimate life

Happy Goal _____

Healthy Goal _____

Wealthy Goal _____

Week starting _____ Accountability Partner Name/# _____

Happy Habits / Actions	Mon	Tues	Wed	Thurs	Fri
_____					
_____					
_____					
_____					
_____					
_____					

Healthy Habits / Actions	Mon	Tues	Wed	Thurs	Fri
_____					
_____					
_____					
_____					
_____					
_____					

Wealthy Habits / Actions	Mon	Tues	Wed	Thurs	Fri
_____					
_____					
_____					
_____					
_____					
_____					

⚙ Committed Habit ☺ Completed Habit ☒ Incomplete Habit ✔ Bonus Habit

WEEKLY TOTAL | 0

Power Up

AFFIRMATIONS

TODAY'S MANTRA

Date ___ / ___
SMTWTFS

TODAY'S THOUGHTS

_____
_____
_____
_____
_____
_____
_____
_____
_____
_____

BRIGHT IDEAS

_____
_____
_____
_____

3 Commitments	Habits	How I Will Lead
H:	Start:	Myself:
H:	Stop:	Others:
W:	Continue:	

Awareness + Action = Wisdom

TOP 3 PRIORITIES

1.

2.

3.

Power Play

Date ___ / ___

SMTWTFS

CALLS:

To make   To return

Time		Time	
6:00		1:00	
6:30		1:30	
7:00		2:00	
7:30		2:30	
8:00		3:00	
8:30		3:30	
9:00		4:00	
9:30		4:30	
10:00		5:00	
10:30		5:30	
11:00		6:00	
11:30		6:30	
12:00		7:00	
12:30		7:30	

Impact

Opportunity

Connection

Stay hydrated!

Step goal: _____   Steps completed: _____   Movement goal: _____

NOTES

_____
_____
_____
_____
_____
_____
_____
_____
_____
_____
_____
_____
_____
_____
_____
_____
_____
_____
_____
_____
_____

To Do	Shopping List	Appointments to Make

Power Down

GRATITUDE

NAILED IT!

REFLECTION

_____
_____
_____
_____
_____
_____
_____
_____
_____
_____

AWARENESS

_____
_____
_____
_____

Commitments Completed	Today's Wins	My HHW Score & Why
H:		H: 1 2 3 4 5
		_____
		_____
H:		H: 1 2 3 4 5
		_____
		_____
W:		W: 1 2 3 4 5
		_____
		_____
		Daily Total: _____

AFFIRMATIONS

Power Up

Date ___ / ___
SMTWTFS

TODAY'S MANTRA

TODAY'S THOUGHTS

_____
_____
_____
_____
_____
_____
_____
_____
_____
_____

BRIGHT IDEAS

_____
_____
_____
_____

3 Commitments	Habits	How I Will Lead
H:	Start:	Myself:
H:	Stop:	
		Others:
W:	Continue:	

The Game is designed to help you evolve and appreciate what is.

TOP 3 PRIORITIES

Power Play

To make   To return

1.

2.

3.

Date ___ / ___
SMTWTFS

6:00	1:00
6:30	1:30
7:00	2:00
7:30	2:30
8:00	3:00
8:30	3:30
9:00	4:00
9:30	4:30
10:00	5:00
10:30	5:30
11:00	6:00
11:30	6:30
12:00	7:00
12:30	7:30

Impact   Opportunity   Connection

Stay hydrated!

Step goal: _____   Steps completed: _____   Movement goal: _____

NOTES

_____
_____
_____
_____
_____
_____
_____
_____
_____
_____
_____
_____
_____
_____
_____
_____
_____
_____
_____
_____
_____
_____

To Do   Shopping List   Appointments to Make

Power Down

GRATITUDE

NAILED IT!

REFLECTION

_____
_____
_____
_____
_____
_____
_____
_____
_____
_____

AWARENESS

_____
_____
_____
_____

Commitments Completed

H:

H:

W:

Today's Wins

My HHW Score & Why

H: 1 2 3 4 5
_____
_____

H: 1 2 3 4 5
_____
_____

W: 1 2 3 4 5
_____
_____

Daily Total: _____

AFFIRMATIONS

Power Up

Date ___ / ___
SMTWTFS

TODAY'S MANTRA

TODAY'S THOUGHTS

_____
_____
_____
_____
_____
_____
_____
_____
_____
_____

BRIGHT IDEAS

_____
_____
_____
_____
_____

3 Commitments	Habits	How I Will Lead
H:	Start:	Myself:
H:	Stop:	
		Others:
W:	Continue:	

Stop and appreciate what you have learned throughout your Game.

TOP 3 PRIORITIES

Power Play

CALLS:
To make   To return

1.

2.

3.

Date ___ / ___
SMTWTFS

6:00 _____	1:00 _____
6:30 _____	1:30 _____
7:00 _____	2:00 _____
7:30 _____	2:30 _____
8:00 _____	3:00 _____
8:30 _____	3:30 _____
9:00 _____	4:00 _____
9:30 _____	4:30 _____
10:00 _____	5:00 _____
10:30 _____	5:30 _____
11:00 _____	6:00 _____
11:30 _____	6:30 _____
12:00 _____	7:00 _____
12:30 _____	7:30 _____

Impact   Opportunity   Connection

Stay hydrated!

Step goal: _____   Steps completed: _____   Movement goal: _____

NOTES

_____

_____

_____

_____

_____

_____

_____

_____

_____

_____

_____

_____

_____

_____

_____

_____

_____

_____

_____

_____

_____

To Do	Shopping List	Appointments to Make

Power Down

GRATITUDE

NAILED IT!

REFLECTION

_____
_____
_____
_____
_____
_____
_____
_____
_____
_____

AWARENESS

_____
_____
_____
_____

Commitments Completed

H:

H:

W:

Today's Wins

My HHW Score & Why

H: 1 2 3 4 5
_____
_____

H: 1 2 3 4 5
_____
_____

W: 1 2 3 4 5
_____
_____

Daily Total: _____

Power Up

AFFIRMATIONS

TODAY'S MANTRA

Date ___ / ___
SMTWTFS

TODAY'S THOUGHTS

_____
_____
_____
_____
_____
_____
_____
_____
_____
_____

BRIGHT IDEAS

_____
_____
_____
_____

3 Commitments	Habits	How I Will Lead
H:	Start:	Myself:
H:	Stop:	
		Others:
W:	Continue:	

*"99 per cent is a b*tch. 100 per cent is a breeze."*
~ Jack Canfield

TOP 3 PRIORITIES

Power Play

CALLS:
To make   To return

Date ___ / ___
SMTWTFS

1.

2.

3.

6:00	1:00
6:30	1:30
7:00	2:00
7:30	2:30
8:00	3:00
8:30	3:30
9:00	4:00
9:30	4:30
10:00	5:00
10:30	5:30
11:00	6:00
11:30	6:30
12:00	7:00
12:30	7:30

Impact   Opportunity   Connection

Stay hydrated!

Step goal: _____   Steps completed: _____   Movement goal: _____

NOTES

_____
_____
_____
_____
_____
_____
_____
_____
_____
_____
_____
_____
_____
_____
_____
_____
_____
_____
_____
_____
_____

To Do	Shopping List	Appointments to Make

Power Down

GRATITUDE

NAILED IT!

REFLECTION

_____
_____
_____
_____
_____
_____
_____
_____
_____
_____

AWARENESS

_____
_____
_____
_____

Commitments Completed	Today's Wins	My HHW Score & Why
H:		H: 1 2 3 4 5
		_____
		_____
H:		H: 1 2 3 4 5
		_____
		_____
W:		W: 1 2 3 4 5
		_____
		_____
		Daily Total: _____

Power Up

AFFIRMATIONS

TODAY'S MANTRA

Date ___ / ___
SMTWTFS

TODAY'S THOUGHTS

_____
_____
_____
_____
_____
_____
_____
_____
_____
_____

BRIGHT IDEAS

_____
_____
_____
_____

3 Commitments	Habits	How I Will Lead
H:	Start:	Myself:
H:	Stop:	
		Others:
W:	Continue:	

"Don't let a good life stop you from living a great life."
~ Jason Borné

TOP 3 PRIORITIES

Power Play

Date ___ / ___
SMTWTFS

CALLS:

To make   To return

1.

2.

3.

6:00	_____	1:00	_____
6:30	_____	1:30	_____
7:00	_____	2:00	_____
7:30	_____	2:30	_____
8:00	_____	3:00	_____
8:30	_____	3:30	_____
9:00	_____	4:00	_____
9:30	_____	4:30	_____
10:00	_____	5:00	_____
10:30	_____	5:30	_____
11:00	_____	6:00	_____
11:30	_____	6:30	_____
12:00	_____	7:00	_____
12:30	_____	7:30	_____

Impact

Opportunity

Connection

Stay hydrated!

Step goal: _____   Steps completed: _____   Movement goal: _____

NOTES

_____
_____
_____
_____
_____
_____
_____
_____
_____
_____
_____
_____
_____
_____
_____
_____
_____
_____
_____
_____
_____

To Do	Shopping List	Appointments to Make

Power Down

GRATITUDE

NAILED IT!

REFLECTION

_____
_____
_____
_____
_____
_____
_____
_____
_____
_____

AWARENESS

_____
_____
_____
_____

Commitments Completed

H:

H:

W:

Today's Wins

My HHW Score & Why

H: 1 2 3 4 5
_____
_____

H: 1 2 3 4 5
_____
_____

W: 1 2 3 4 5
_____
_____

Daily Total: _____

AFFIRMATIONS

Power Up

Date ___ / ___
SMTWTFS

TODAY'S MANTRA

TODAY'S THOUGHTS

_____
_____
_____
_____
_____
_____
_____
_____
_____

BRIGHT IDEAS

_____
_____
_____
_____

3 Commitments	Habits	How I Will Lead
H:	Start:	Myself:
H:	Stop:	
W:	Continue:	Others:

"Remember, it's your choice to create your Ultimate Life!"
~ Jim Bunch

TOP 3 PRIORITIES

Power Play

CALLS:
To make   To return

1.

2.

3.

Date ___ / ___
SMTWTFS

6:00	1:00
6:30	1:30
7:00	2:00
7:30	2:30
8:00	3:00
8:30	3:30
9:00	4:00
9:30	4:30
10:00	5:00
10:30	5:30
11:00	6:00
11:30	6:30
12:00	7:00
12:30	7:30

Impact   Opportunity   Connection

Stay hydrated!

Step goal: _____   Steps completed: _____   Movement goal: _____

NOTES

_____

_____

_____

_____

_____

_____

_____

_____

_____

_____

_____

_____

_____

_____

_____

_____

_____

_____

_____

_____

To Do	Shopping List	Appointments to Make

Power Down

GRATITUDE

NAILED IT!

REFLECTION

_____
_____
_____
_____
_____
_____
_____
_____
_____
_____

AWARENESS

_____
_____
_____
_____

Commitments Completed	Today's Wins	My HHW Score & Why
H:		H: 1 2 3 4 5
		_____
		_____
H:		H: 1 2 3 4 5
		_____
		_____
W:		W: 1 2 3 4 5
		_____
		_____
		Daily Total: _____

Power Up

AFFIRMATIONS

Date ___ / ___
SMTWTFS

TODAY'S MANTRA

TODAY'S THOUGHTS

_____
_____
_____
_____
_____
_____
_____
_____
_____
_____

BRIGHT IDEAS

_____
_____
_____
_____

3 Commitments	Habits	How I Will Lead
H:	Start:	Myself:
H:	Stop:	
W:	Continue:	Others:

"I took the leap, and I'm not looking back."
~ Gina Pigott

TOP 3 PRIORITIES

1.

2.

3.

Power Play

Date ___ / ___
SMTWTFS

CALLS:

To make   To return

Time		Time	
6:00	_____	1:00	_____
6:30	_____	1:30	_____
7:00	_____	2:00	_____
7:30	_____	2:30	_____
8:00	_____	3:00	_____
8:30	_____	3:30	_____
9:00	_____	4:00	_____
9:30	_____	4:30	_____
10:00	_____	5:00	_____
10:30	_____	5:30	_____
11:00	_____	6:00	_____
11:30	_____	6:30	_____
12:00	_____	7:00	_____
12:30	_____	7:30	_____

Impact

Opportunity

Connection

Stay hydrated!

Step goal: _____   Steps completed: _____   Movement goal: _____

NOTES

_____

_____

_____

_____

_____

_____

_____

_____

_____

_____

_____

_____

_____

_____

_____

_____

_____

_____

_____

_____

_____

To Do	Shopping List	Appointments to Make

Power Down

GRATITUDE

NAILED IT!

REFLECTION

_____
_____
_____
_____
_____
_____
_____
_____
_____
_____

AWARENESS

_____
_____
_____
_____

Commitments Completed	Today's Wins	My HHW Score & Why
H:		H: 1 2 3 4 5
		_____
		_____
H:		H: 1 2 3 4 5
		_____
		_____
W:		W: 1 2 3 4 5
		_____
		_____
		Daily Total: _____

Victory Lap

_____

_____

_____

_____

_____

_____

_____

_____

_____

_____

_____

_____

_____

_____

_____

_____

_____

_____

_____

_____

_____

_____

_____

Wins

_____
_____
_____
_____
_____
_____
_____
_____
_____
_____
_____
_____
_____
_____
_____
_____
_____
_____
_____
_____
_____
_____
_____
_____
_____
_____
_____

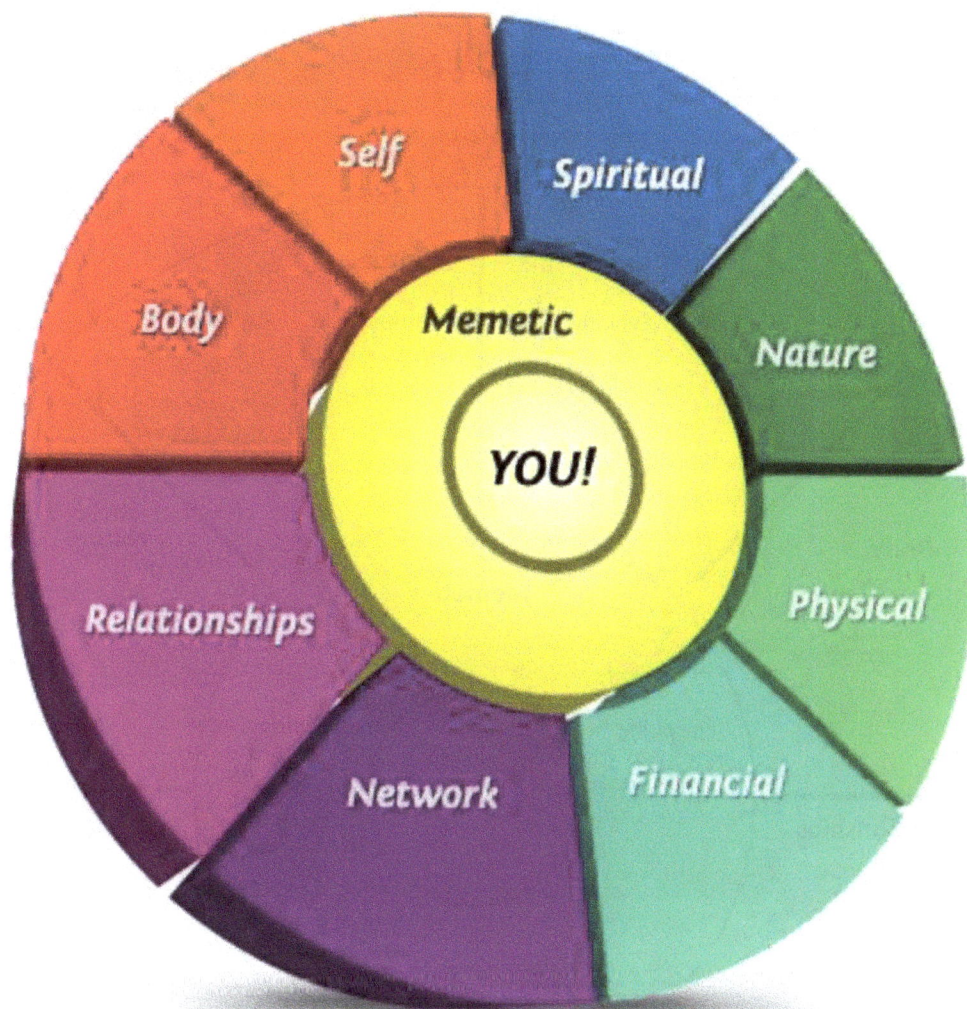

9 Environments of You Wheel
© 2005 CoachVille, LLC
Used with Permission

ultimate life

- Identify at least 3 items for each environment that inspire you.

-Identify at least 3 items for each environment that expire you.

Self

Inspiring | Expiring

Spiritual

Inspiring | Expiring

Body

Inspiring | Expiring

Nature

Inspiring | Expiring

Memetics

Inspiring | Expiring

Relationships

Inspiring | Expiring

Physical

Inspiring | Expiring

Network

Inspiring | Expiring

Financial

Inspiring | Expiring

Copyright 2008 – 2021 – All Rights Reserved
The Ultimate Game of Life
Happy Healthy Wealthy Game

THE ULTIMATE 9 WEEK PLANNER
DESIGN YOUR HAPPY HEALTHY WEALTHY LIFE

Before ~ After

_____

_____

_____

_____

_____

_____

_____

_____

_____

_____

_____

_____

_____

_____

_____

_____

_____

_____

_____

_____

_____

_____

_____

_____

_____

What's Next

_____

_____

_____

_____

_____

_____

_____

_____

_____

_____

_____

_____

_____

_____

_____

_____

_____

_____

_____

_____

_____

_____

_____

_____

_____

Healthy and Wealthy Trackers

Financial Tracker

	EXPENSES/SPENDING	INCOME	SAVINGS	UPCOMING BILLS
WEEK 1		Active Passive		
WEEK 2		Active Passive		
WEEK 3		Active Passive		
WEEK 4		Active Passive		
WEEK 5		Active Passive		
WEEK 6		Active Passive		
WEEK 7		Active Passive		
WEEK 8		Active Passive		
WEEK 9		Active Passive		

Nutrition Tracker

DAY & **DATE** _____ S M T W T F S

MEAL

SNACK

MEAL

SNACK

MEAL

Supplements: ☐   Enzymes: ☐

FAST   Start Time: _____   Stop Time: _____

DAY & **DATE** _____ S M T W T F S

MEAL

SNACK

MEAL

SNACK

MEAL

Supplements: ☐   Enzymes: ☐

FAST   Start Time: _____   Stop Time: _____

DAY & **DATE** _____ S M T W T F S

MEAL

SNACK

MEAL

SNACK

MEAL

Supplements: ☐   Enzymes: ☐

FAST   Start Time: _____   Stop Time: _____

DAY & **DATE** _____ S M T W T F S

MEAL

SNACK

MEAL

SNACK

MEAL

Supplements: ☐   Enzymes: ☐

FAST   Start Time: _____   Stop Time: _____

Nutrition Tracker

DAY & DATE _____ S M T W T F S

MEAL

SNACK

MEAL

SNACK

MEAL

Supplements: ▢   Enzymes: ▢

FAST Start Time: _____ Stop Time: _____

DAY & DATE _____ S M T W T F S

MEAL

SNACK

MEAL

SNACK

MEAL

Supplements: ▢   Enzymes: ▢

FAST Start Time: _____ Stop Time: _____

DAY & DATE _____ S M T W T F S

MEAL

SNACK

MEAL

SNACK

MEAL

Supplements: ▢   Enzymes: ▢

FAST Start Time: _____ Stop Time: _____

WEEKLY REVIEW

Weight: _____   Body Fat %: _____

Other: _____

_____

Fitness Mins: __ __ __ __ __ __ __

Hours Slept: __ __ __ __ __ __ __

Aerobic   Core   Cycling

Sports   Strength   Swimming

Martial Arts   Meditation   Yoga

Other _____   Other _____

Nutrition Tracker

DAY & DATE _____ S M T W T F S

MEAL

SNACK

MEAL

SNACK

MEAL

Supplements: [ ]   Enzymes: [ ]

FAST Start Time: _____   Stop Time: _____

DAY & DATE _____ S M T W T F S

MEAL

SNACK

MEAL

SNACK

MEAL

Supplements: [ ]   Enzymes: [ ]

FAST Start Time: _____   Stop Time: _____

DAY & DATE _____ S M T W T F S

MEAL

SNACK

MEAL

SNACK

MEAL

Supplements: [ ]   Enzymes: [ ]

FAST Start Time: _____   Stop Time: _____

DAY & DATE _____ S M T W T F S

MEAL

SNACK

MEAL

SNACK

MEAL

Supplements: [ ]   Enzymes: [ ]

FAST Start Time: _____   Stop Time: _____

Nutrition Tracker

DAY & DATE _____ S M T W T F S

MEAL

SNACK

MEAL

SNACK

MEAL

Supplements: ☐   Enzymes: ☐

FAST Start Time: _____ Stop Time: _____

DAY & DATE _____ S M T W T F S

MEAL

SNACK

MEAL

SNACK

MEAL

Supplements: ☐   Enzymes: ☐

FAST Start Time: _____ Stop Time: _____

DAY & DATE _____ S M T W T F S

MEAL

SNACK

MEAL

SNACK

MEAL

Supplements: ☐   Enzymes: ☐

FAST Start Time: _____ Stop Time: _____

WEEKLY REVIEW

🏋 Weight: _____   📏 Body Fat %: _____

Other: _____

_____

Fitness Mins: ___ ___ ___ ___ ___ ___ ___

Hours Slept: ___ ___ ___ ___ ___ ___ ___

🏃 Aerobic ☐   🏋 Core ☐   🚲 Cycling ☐

🏈 Sports ☐   🏋 Strength ☐   🏊 Swimming ☐

🥋 Martial Arts ☐   🧘 Meditation ☐   🧘 Yoga ☐

Other _____ ☐   Other _____ ☐

Nutrition Tracker

DAY & DATE _____ S M T W T F S

MEAL

SNACK

MEAL

SNACK

MEAL

Supplements: ____ Enzymes: ____

FAST

Start Time: _____ Stop Time: _____

DAY & DATE _____ S M T W T F S

MEAL

SNACK

MEAL

SNACK

MEAL

Supplements: ____ Enzymes: ____

FAST

Start Time: _____ Stop Time: _____

DAY & DATE _____ S M T W T F S

MEAL

SNACK

MEAL

SNACK

MEAL

Supplements: ____ Enzymes: ____

FAST

Start Time: _____ Stop Time: _____

DAY & DATE _____ S M T W T F S

MEAL

SNACK

MEAL

SNACK

MEAL

Supplements: ____ Enzymes: ____

FAST

Start Time: _____ Stop Time: _____

Nutrition Tracker

DAY & DATE _____ S M T W T F S

MEAL

SNACK

MEAL

SNACK

MEAL

Supplements: ☐   Enzymes: ☐

FAST Start Time: _____ Stop Time: _____

DAY & DATE _____ S M T W T F S

MEAL

SNACK

MEAL

SNACK

MEAL

Supplements: ☐   Enzymes: ☐

FAST Start Time: _____ Stop Time: _____

DAY & DATE _____ S M T W T F S

MEAL

SNACK

MEAL

SNACK

MEAL

Supplements: ☐   Enzymes: ☐

FAST Start Time: _____ Stop Time: _____

WEEKLY REVIEW

Weight: _____   Body Fat %: _____

Other: _____

_____

Fitness Mins: __ __ __ __ __ __ __

Hours Slept: __ __ __ __ __ __ __

🏃 Aerobic ☐   🏋 Core ☐   🚲 Cycling ☐

🏈 Sports ☐   🏋 Strength ☐   🏊 Swimming ☐

🥋 Martial Arts ☐   🧘 Meditation ☐   🧘 Yoga ☐

Other _____ ☐   Other _____ ☐

Nutrition Tracker

DAY & DATE _____ **S M T W T F S**

MEAL

SNACK

MEAL

SNACK

MEAL

FAST

Supplements: ☐   Enzymes: ☐

Start Time: _____   Stop Time: _____

DAY & DATE _____ **S M T W T F S**

MEAL

SNACK

MEAL

SNACK

MEAL

FAST

Supplements: ☐   Enzymes: ☐

Start Time: _____   Stop Time: _____

DAY & DATE _____ **S M T W T F S**

MEAL

SNACK

MEAL

SNACK

MEAL

FAST

Supplements: ☐   Enzymes: ☐

Start Time: _____   Stop Time: _____

DAY & DATE _____ **S M T W T F S**

MEAL

SNACK

MEAL

SNACK

MEAL

FAST

Supplements: ☐   Enzymes: ☐

Start Time: _____   Stop Time: _____

Nutrition Tracker

DAY & DATE _____ S M T W T F S

MEAL

SNACK

MEAL

SNACK

MEAL

Supplements: ☐   Enzymes: ☐

FAST Start Time: _____   Stop Time: _____

DAY & DATE _____ S M T W T F S

MEAL

SNACK

MEAL

SNACK

MEAL

Supplements: ☐   Enzymes: ☐

FAST Start Time: _____   Stop Time: _____

DAY & DATE _____ S M T W T F S

MEAL

SNACK

MEAL

SNACK

MEAL

Supplements: ☐   Enzymes: ☐

FAST Start Time: _____   Stop Time: _____

WEEKLY REVIEW

Weight: _____   Body Fat %: _____

Other: _____

_____

Fitness Mins: __ __ __ __ __ __ __

Hours Slept: __ __ __ __ __ __ __

☐ Aerobic   ☐ Core   ☐ Cycling

☐ Sports   ☐ Strength   ☐ Swimming

☐ Martial Arts   ☐ Meditation ☐ Yoga

Other _____   Other _____

Nutrition Tracker

DAY & DATE _____ S M T W T F S

MEAL

SNACK

MEAL

SNACK

MEAL

Supplements: ☐   Enzymes: ☐

FAST Start Time: _____ Stop Time: _____

DAY & DATE _____ S M T W T F S

MEAL

SNACK

MEAL

SNACK

MEAL

Supplements: ☐   Enzymes: ☐

FAST Start Time: _____ Stop Time: _____

DAY & DATE _____ S M T W T F S

MEAL

SNACK

MEAL

SNACK

MEAL

Supplements: ☐   Enzymes: ☐

FAST Start Time: _____ Stop Time: _____

DAY & DATE _____ S M T W T F S

MEAL

SNACK

MEAL

SNACK

MEAL

Supplements: ☐   Enzymes: ☐

FAST Start Time: _____ Stop Time: _____

Nutrition Tracker

DAY & DATE _____ S M T W T F S

MEAL

SNACK

MEAL

SNACK

MEAL

Supplements: ☐   Enzymes: ☐

FAST Start Time: _____   Stop Time: _____

DAY & DATE _____ S M T W T F S

MEAL

SNACK

MEAL

SNACK

MEAL

Supplements: ☐   Enzymes: ☐

FAST Start Time: _____   Stop Time: _____

DAY & DATE _____ S M T W T F S

MEAL

SNACK

MEAL

SNACK

MEAL

Supplements: ☐   Enzymes: ☐

FAST Start Time: _____   Stop Time: _____

WEEKLY REVIEW

Weight: _____   Body Fat %: _____

Other: _____

_____

Fitness Mins: ___ ___ ___ ___ ___ ___ ___

Hours Slept: ___ ___ ___ ___ ___ ___ ___

Aerobic ☐   Core ☐   Cycling ☐

Sports ☐   Strength ☐   Swimming ☐

Martial Arts ☐   Meditation ☐   Yoga ☐

Other _____ ☐   Other _____ ☐

Nutrition Tracker

DAY & DATE _____ S M T W T F S

MEAL

SNACK

MEAL

SNACK

MEAL

Supplements: ☐   Enzymes: ☐

FAST Start Time: _____ Stop Time: _____

DAY & DATE _____ S M T W T F S

MEAL

SNACK

MEAL

SNACK

MEAL

Supplements: ☐   Enzymes: ☐

FAST Start Time: _____ Stop Time: _____

DAY & DATE _____ S M T W T F S

MEAL

SNACK

MEAL

SNACK

MEAL

Supplements: ☐   Enzymes: ☐

FAST Start Time: _____ Stop Time: _____

DAY & DATE _____ S M T W T F S

MEAL

SNACK

MEAL

SNACK

MEAL

Supplements: ☐   Enzymes: ☐

FAST Start Time: _____ Stop Time: _____

Nutrition Tracker

DAY & DATE _____ S M T W T F S

MEAL

SNACK

MEAL

SNACK

MEAL

Supplements: ___   Enzymes: ___

FAST Start Time: _____   Stop Time: _____

DAY & DATE _____ S M T W T F S

MEAL

SNACK

MEAL

SNACK

MEAL

Supplements: ___   Enzymes: ___

FAST Start Time: _____   Stop Time: _____

DAY & DATE _____ S M T W T F S

MEAL

SNACK

MEAL

SNACK

MEAL

Supplements: ___   Enzymes: ___

FAST Start Time: _____   Stop Time: _____

WEEKLY REVIEW

Weight: _____   Body Fat %: _____

Other: _____

_____

Fitness Mins: ___ ___ ___ ___ ___ ___ ___

Hours Slept: ___ ___ ___ ___ ___ ___ ___

Aerobic ___   Core ___   Cycling ___

Sports ___   Strength ___   Swimming ___

Martial Arts ___   Meditation ___   Yoga ___

Other _____   Other _____

Nutrition Tracker

DAY & DATE _____ S M T W T F S

MEAL

SNACK

MEAL

SNACK

MEAL

Supplements: ☐   Enzymes: ☐

FAST   Start Time: _____   Stop Time: _____

DAY & DATE _____ S M T W T F S

MEAL

SNACK

MEAL

SNACK

MEAL

Supplements: ☐   Enzymes: ☐

FAST   Start Time: _____   Stop Time: _____

DAY & DATE _____ S M T W T F S

MEAL

SNACK

MEAL

SNACK

MEAL

Supplements: ☐   Enzymes: ☐

FAST   Start Time: _____   Stop Time: _____

DAY & DATE _____ S M T W T F S

MEAL

SNACK

MEAL

SNACK

MEAL

Supplements: ☐   Enzymes: ☐

FAST   Start Time: _____   Stop Time: _____

Nutrition Tracker

DAY & DATE _____ S M T W T F S

MEAL

SNACK

MEAL

SNACK

MEAL

Supplements: ☐   Enzymes: ☐

FAST Start Time: _____ Stop Time: _____

DAY & DATE _____ S M T W T F S

MEAL

SNACK

MEAL

SNACK

MEAL

Supplements: ☐   Enzymes: ☐

FAST Start Time: _____ Stop Time: _____

DAY & DATE _____ S M T W T F S

MEAL

SNACK

MEAL

SNACK

MEAL

Supplements: ☐   Enzymes: ☐

FAST Start Time: _____ Stop Time: _____

WEEKLY REVIEW

Weight: _____   Body Fat %: _____

Other: _____

_____

Fitness Mins: __ __ __ __ __ __ __

Hours Slept: __ __ __ __ __ __ __

Aerobic ☐   Core ☐   Cycling ☐

Sports ☐   Strength ☐   Swimming ☐

Martial Arts ☐   Meditation ☐   Yoga ☐

Other _____ ☐   Other _____

Nutrition Tracker

DAY & **DATE** _____ S M T W T F S

MEAL

SNACK

MEAL

SNACK

MEAL

Supplements: ☐ Enzymes: ☐

FAST

Start Time: _____ Stop Time: _____

DAY & **DATE** _____ S M T W T F S

MEAL

SNACK

MEAL

SNACK

MEAL

Supplements: ☐ Enzymes: ☐

FAST

Start Time: _____ Stop Time: _____

DAY & **DATE** _____ S M T W T F S

MEAL

SNACK

MEAL

SNACK

MEAL

Supplements: ☐ Enzymes: ☐

FAST

Start Time: _____ Stop Time: _____

DAY & **DATE** _____ S M T W T F S

MEAL

SNACK

MEAL

SNACK

MEAL

Supplements: ☐ Enzymes: ☐

FAST

Start Time: _____ Stop Time: _____

Nutrition Tracker

DAY & **DATE** _____ S M T W T F S

MEAL

SNACK

MEAL

SNACK

MEAL

Supplements: Enzymes:

FAST   Start Time: _____   Stop Time: _____

DAY & **DATE** _____ S M T W T F S

MEAL

SNACK

MEAL

SNACK

MEAL

Supplements: Enzymes:

FAST   Start Time: _____   Stop Time: _____

DAY & **DATE** _____ S M T W T F S

MEAL

SNACK

MEAL

SNACK

MEAL

Supplements: Enzymes:

FAST   Start Time: _____   Stop Time: _____

WEEKLY REVIEW

🏋 Weight: _____   🏷 Body Fat %: _____

Other: _____

_____

Fitness Mins: ___ ___ ___ ___ ___ ___ ___

Hours Slept: ___ ___ ___ ___ ___ ___ ___

🏃 Aerobic   🧘 Core   🚲 Cycling

🏈 Sports   🏋 Strength   🏊 Swimming

🥋 Martial Arts   🪨 Meditation   🧘 Yoga

Other _____   Other _____

Nutrition Tracker

DAY & DATE _____ S M T W T F S

MEAL

SNACK

MEAL

SNACK

MEAL

Supplements: ☐   Enzymes: ☐

FAST Start Time: _____ Stop Time: _____

DAY & DATE _____ S M T W T F S

MEAL

SNACK

MEAL

SNACK

MEAL

Supplements: ☐   Enzymes: ☐

FAST Start Time: _____ Stop Time: _____

DAY & DATE _____ S M T W T F S

MEAL

SNACK

MEAL

SNACK

MEAL

Supplements: ☐   Enzymes: ☐

FAST Start Time: _____ Stop Time: _____

DAY & DATE _____ S M T W T F S

MEAL

SNACK

MEAL

SNACK

MEAL

Supplements: ☐   Enzymes: ☐

FAST Start Time: _____ Stop Time: _____

Nutrition Tracker

DAY & DATE _____ S M T W T F S

MEAL

SNACK

MEAL

SNACK

MEAL

Supplements: ____ Enzymes: ____

FAST Start Time: _____ Stop Time: _____

DAY & DATE _____ S M T W T F S

MEAL

SNACK

MEAL

SNACK

MEAL

Supplements: ____ Enzymes: ____

FAST Start Time: _____ Stop Time: _____

DAY & DATE _____ S M T W T F S

MEAL

SNACK

MEAL

SNACK

MEAL

Supplements: ____ Enzymes: ____

FAST Start Time: _____ Stop Time: _____

WEEKLY REVIEW

Weight: _____   Body Fat %: _____

Other: _____

_____

Fitness Mins: __ __ __ __ __ __ __

Hours Slept: __ __ __ __ __ __ __

Aerobic   Core   Cycling

Sports   Strength   Swimming

Martial Arts   Meditation   Yoga

Other _____   Other _____

ABOUT THE AUTHOR

Gina is a successful serial entrepreneur, who has spearheaded multiple businesses for the past two decades.

She has a passion for helping others and is always willing to take on a new challenge. To that end, she is a business coach and consultant focusing on Career Coaching, Leadership Development and Cultural Transformation, and she recently launched two teams that work with small- and medium-sized businesses on cultural alignment, process streamlining and fiscal growth and stability. Gina's strengths include creating a positive cultural environment geared to success.

Gina's motto is: It's all about choices! She's a firm believer that you can always change your life. So she has taken on the role of CEO of Ultimate Life Technologies, LLC, partnering with Jim Bunch in guiding his team of coaches and players who are looking to level up their lives. In her multi-faceted role as CEO, Player and Team Coach, Gina leads the team in setting and achieving goals through action. Gina is also certified by The Barrett Values Centre in their Cultural Transformation Tools and by The Canfield Organization in Jack Canfield's Success Principles.

A true inspiration for those that work with her, Gina is down-to-earth, straightforward, and consistently finds a way to assist people in finding the best in themselves and those they lead.

Gina values family; she shares her life with her partner Paulie, 5 children Joseph, Kayla, Michael, Lani and Noelle, 3 dogs, chickens and ducks. When she's not working, she's cooking. Gina aspires to Rock Life surrounded by family, friends and music.